Healing Guides
Align Your Signs

THE ASTROLOGY OF
RELATIONSHIPS

Published in 2024
First published in the UK by SparkPool Publishing
An imprint of Igloo Books Ltd
Cottage Farm, NN6 0BJ, UK
Owned by Bonnier Books
Sveavägen 56, Stockholm, Sweden
www.igloobooks.com

0824 001
2 4 6 8 10 9 7 5 3 1
ISBN 978-1-83795-616-6

Cover illustrated by Suzanne Washington
Written by Em Bruce

Designed by Simon Parker
Edited by Cameron-Rose Neal

Printed and manufactured in China

CONTENTS

Introduction 4

How to Use This Book 6

Aries 8

Taurus 15

Gemini 22

Cancer 29

Leo 36

Virgo... 43

Libra 50

Scorpio 57

Sagittarius 64

Capricorn 71

Aquarius 78

Pisces 85

Conclusion 92

INTRODUCTION

There's no doubt about it, astrology's having a moment – and it's not hard to understand why. Navigating relationships has never been more complicated, what with the deluge of dating apps available, endless swiping and cheesy bios. Love, friendships and relationships with family and colleagues can often feel like wandering through uncharted territory, with unexpected twists, turns and the odd patch of quicksand along the way. So, it's no wonder that – just as our ancestors used the stars to navigate – more and more of us are turning to astrology to help us chart a smooth course through life.

We human beings have sought the help of celestial forces to better understand ourselves and those around us for millennia. Whether we're turning to community elders for advice or consulting ancient scripture, the search for meaning is a common thread that connects us to everyone alive today, and everyone who came before us. Archaeological evidence suggests that astrology is one of the earliest systems developed by ancient civilisations to find meaning in the present and anticipate the future. It offers a method of interpreting, steering and improving our relationships, giving us a greater sense of certainty in an increasingly uncertain world. So, whether you're seeking to strengthen existing bonds or embark on new adventures in love and friendship, this book will show you how you can use astrology as a cosmic compass to guide your journey to harmonious and fulfilling connections.

This guide is designed for both astrology newbies and seasoned stargazers alike, so we'll start by looking at the role of astrology in the modern era and bust some myths about what astrology can and can't do for a relationship, then dive right into how you can use this book to better understand your relationships. Let's get started!

The modern astrologists

While astrology has fascinating, ancient roots, it has evolved significantly throughout the 20th and 21st centuries into the contemporary practice we know today.

Astrology's meteoric rise in popularity is thanks, in part, to a marked shift in social attitudes towards our quest for self-discovery, self-actualisation and spiritual fulfilment. In recent years, astrology has also undergone a particularly radical transformation in the digital realm, where those seeking cosmic guidance can access personal horoscopes, detailed birth charts and a whole community of like-minded truth-seekers at the touch of a button.

A quick scroll through astrology hashtags online is all the proof you need that modern astrologists have successfully combined the power of the cosmos with the power of social media – arguably two of the greatest forces in the universe – to reach a global audience and make astrology more accessible, customisable and fashionable than ever before. Modern astrologists have blended our timeless search for meaning with our contemporary search for enlightenment and empowerment in modern relationships.

What astrology is (and what it isn't)

In the broadest sense, astrology is the human search for meaning in the sky. Astrology seeks to find connections between the movements of the stars and planets and our behaviours, personalities and actions here on Earth. However, while astrology allows us to discern patterns between the stars and ourselves – and to observe and anticipate likely events – it's important to understand that it cannot exactly predict the future (and really, where would be the fun in that?).

And last, but definitely not least, astrology is *not* astronomy. Astronomy is the scientific study of the universe; it's the realm of Big Bangs and black holes, gas giants and Galileo. So, if you're at a party and someone asks you if you're into astronomy, don't whip out your birth chart. You've been warned.

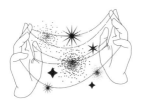

HOW TO USE THIS BOOK

This book will show you how you can put astrology to work in your relationships. Whether it's figuring out how best to schmooze a new co-worker, recognising when your roommate needs a bit of space or giving you the nudge to finally ask for that cute barista's number – astrology is about to become your ultimate relationship wingman.

You'll delve into compatibility between the zodiac signs, discover which signs you're most likely to gel with in your personal, professional and romantic relationships and learn how best to navigate your relationships with the signs you might be cosmically inclined to clash with.

In your element

You might already know a little bit about the zodiac sign you were born under and the common personality traits of those who share your sign; but did you know that each of the twelve signs are also associated with one of four elements? That's right, each zodiac sign belongs to either fire, water, earth or air, and the characteristics of these elements can help you understand your own and others' approach to life and relationships.

When it comes to compatibility, signs within the same element are generally more likely to get on like an astrological house on fire, but that's not to say that a relationship with someone from a different element can't also be full of sparks. You'll look at compatibility between the signs and elements in more detail throughout this book, but here's a quick introduction to get you started.

Fire — Aries, Leo and Sagittarius

These fiery signs can be hard to resist, with their warm and lively personalities drawing people to them like moths to a flame. As partners, fire signs are usually dynamic, passionate, inspiring and energising, and they'll always be on the lookout for ways to light a fire under the relationship.

Air — Gemini, Libra and Aquarius

Air signs tend to gravitate towards each other because the air element thrives on communication and connection. These sociable and easy-breezy signs always have plenty to talk about, so if you're looking for stimulating conversation with a partner who is curious and interested in the world, then love might just be in the air.

Earth — Taurus, Virgo and Capricorn

Earth signs tend to be dependable, practical and commitment-minded. They thrive when they're working together to make plans and see them through, and their loyalty is unshakeable. As partners, earth signs are willing to put a lot of effort into making a relationship stand the test of time.

Water — Cancer, Scorpio and Pisces

Emotional and highly intuitive, there's not much you can get past a water sign. There's something undeniably alluring about their mysterious and secretive nature, so it's no wonder they make for intense and passionate partners. In relationships, water signs value strong connections and know how to create lasting bonds.

Your cosmic guide

Perhaps you're a deep-feeling Cancer who's about to discover that sensitivity is your relationship superpower? Maybe you're a diplomatic Libra looking to use your natural communication skills to create relationship harmony? Or perhaps you're a hot-headed Aries who's keen to learn how to channel your impulsive nature into some spontaneous romance? Whatever your starting point, this book will guide you through how you can use your new astrological knowledge to better understand yourself and your relationships and navigate them with authenticity, confidence and calm. So, are you ready to find out what's written in the stars for your relationships? Of course you are!

Please note – the dates of the zodiac can fluctuate as the alignment of the stars shift due to the moon's gravitational pull on Earth. The dates in this book were correct at the time of writing.

ARIES
21st March – 19th April

ARIES FACT FILE

Element: Fire

Symbol: The ram

Ruling planet: Mars

Colour: Fiery red

Key traits: Energetic, assertive, independent, bold, adventurous, brave, driven and ambitious

Strengths: Leadership, enthusiasm, self-belief, spontaneity and forward-thinking

Weaknesses: Impatience, impulsiveness and tendency to be headstrong and overly competitive

Likes: New challenges, adventures and taking charge of their destiny

Dislikes: Boredom, delays and remaining idle

Meet Aries

The first sign of the zodiac, Aries was certainly at the front of the queue when they were handing out boldness. With plenty of natural confidence, Aries charges horns-first at life at a million miles an hour. Fiercely independent and brimming with enviable self-belief, Aries forges their own path, head-butting obstacles out of the way without a second thought. (This could also explain why Aries is the most accident-prone sign in the zodiac. Please look before you head-butt, Aries.) But despite their feisty nature, Aries also has an unwavering enthusiasm that gives an endearing edge to their somewhat intimidating presence. So, helmets on for a fast-paced, no-holds 'baa-ed' guide to everything you need to know about the fiery ram, Aries.

If you're an Aries...

There's no doubt about it, you're one of life's great doers. You get things done and then you swiftly move on to the next thing. Who has time to hang around, right?

Well, as it turns out, there's a lot you miss when you're travelling at a hundred miles an hour. Like other people, for example. Yes, it's true, you can get a bit one-track-minded and sometimes lose sight of those around you. Your enthusiasm is infectious and it's one of the reasons people are so drawn to you – but try not to get carried away and remember to give other people a chance to be heard, too.

Your way of connecting with others is through action, making plans and doing things. You're super competitive, so high-octane activities that involve an element of competition are likely to be your go-to. But not everyone shares your competitive spirit, so try mixing it up with some slower-paced activities where you can really connect with your loved ones – like taking your bestie to a cooking class, inviting your neighbour for a stroll around the local market or treating your mum to a latte at that new coffee shop she told you about.

When it comes to communication, you're not one for beating around the bush. But if you're not careful, this direct style can get you into hot water. Try taking a step back to observe other people's communication styles and mirror them when you interact – it doesn't mean they're right and you're wrong, but you'll find you get a lot further when you're speaking the same language.

Your Aries mantra:
'SLOW IT DOWN.'

As the speediest sign in the zodiac, you tend to have a 'leap before you look' approach to life. Your fire burns bright but taking on too much can leave you at risk of burnout. Repeat this mantra to remind yourself that patience is a virtue.

If you know an Aries...

If you're lucky enough to have a fiery Aries in your life – or if you're hoping to soon – you might be wondering how best to navigate your relationship with this powerhouse of a personality.

Whether you want to strengthen an existing relationship with an Aries or strike up a new one, the key word is action. Just because Aries are natural leaders, doesn't mean they want to always have to be the one to instigate an activity, project or catch-up. They're drawn to other go-getter personalities, so be proactive and make the first move. Try inviting the Aries in your life on an active adventure, like an outdoor treasure hunt, a hike or a round of crazy golf. Not an outdoorsy person? No worries! Any activity where you're constantly moving forward or progressing – like a trivia night, escape room or bar hopping – will go down a treat with your energetic Aries. (Plus, taking the reins every once in a while will remind your Aries that they're not the only one with great ideas!)

When you need to have an important or tricky conversation with an Aries, the secret to success is getting straight to the point. Nuance and subtlety will likely be lost on Aries, so be clear and direct about what you want. Even if this doesn't come naturally to you, the Aries in your life will appreciate this no-frills approach way more than if you dance around the issue.

Your mantra for connecting with an Aries:
'HOLD ON TIGHT.'

Trying to keep up with an Aries can feel like trying to board a runaway train, but once you get on the same track, you'll love every second of the journey (even if your hair gets a bit windswept in the process). So, embrace the rambunctious ram in your life and hold on tight – the ride will be worth it.

Heavenly matches with Aries

As with all signs, Aries tends to vibe best with the others in their element – in this case, that's the fellow fire signs, Leo and Sagittarius. But fire signs are also stoked by the billowing winds of air signs, and that's exactly where Aries finds one of their most heavenly matches in the zodiac.

Leo, Sagittarius and Gemini

When it comes to confidence, Aries is perhaps second only to Leo, and these two together can seem like an unshakeable force of nature – once they learn how to take turns sharing the limelight, that is! Bold Aries is also drawn to adventurous Sagittarius, and this pair shares an endless curiosity and joie de vivre. They'll also often share many similar hobbies and interests and, whether it's as new friends or romantic partners, they'll slot seamlessly into each other's lives.

Outside of the fire element, one particularly potent pairing is Aries and Gemini. Aries and Gemini both live on the fast, playful and carefree side of life and their celestial chemistry is undeniable and enviable. Once these two team up, there's no separating them.

Aries and you

Having an Aries in your life is like having a human sparkler with you everywhere you go. They're dynamic, fun, fearless and guaranteed to draw a crowd. So how do you keep your relationship with Aries glowing bright if you're not a Leo, Sagittarius or Gemini?

Like all fire signs, Aries has an energetic and lively personality that naturally attracts people to them so, no matter your sign, if you have a similarly bold, free-spirited or action-oriented personality, you'll be sure to feel the spark with Aries. Remember, Aries values action and ambition, so if you've got a dream, passion or the drive to make your mark on the world – no matter how big or small – share it with the Aries in your life and watch them become your biggest cheerleader on the road to success.

Cosmic clashes with Aries

While relationships between some signs seem to be written in the stars, other pairings can struggle to find their rhythm. Aries' bold nature can clash with more sensitive and reserved personalities, which tend to be found in the water and earth elements.

Cancer, Pisces and Virgo

Aries' trademark direct communication style can run the risk of unintentionally offending sensitive souls who are more emotionally attuned, like water signs Cancer and Pisces. This could be particularly evident in romantic relationships and high-pressure work environments. And while ambitious Aries always has things to do and places to be, daydreamers like Pisces prefer to go with the flow and see what the tide brings, so compromise will be the key to harmony for this pair.

There aren't many who can keep up with million-miles-an-hour Aries, and those who enjoy a more peaceful pace of life may struggle to handle Aries' boundless energy. This is often true of the more grounded earth signs like Virgo, who thrive on stability and order.

Finding harmony

One of the biggest sources of discord in relationships with an Aries is a clash of communication styles. Aries values directness: they tend to say it exactly as it is. If you're looking for someone to sugarcoat a tricky conversation, you probably don't want to call on an Aries. Of course, this is just because their priority is getting to the point as quickly as possible (classic Aries), but they often forget that not everyone likes to communicate this way. This also means that subtext may be lost on them (so if you're waiting for Aries to pick up on your subtle hints, you could be waiting a long time!). The flip side of this is that if you need to address an issue you're having with the Aries in your life, having an open, upfront conversation with them in their own direct style is the best first step towards a harmonious outcome.

Charting a smooth course as an Aries

Patience, subtlety and emotional dexterity might not be at the top of the list when it comes to your many admirable traits, Aries, but they're all crucial for creating harmony in your personal and professional relationships. So, how can a hot-headed ram like you navigate relationships with people you might be more likely to lock horns with?

As an Aries, you have a reputation for being a tad impatient and impulsive. These traits can often cause sparks to fly, especially in the workplace, where you may be working alongside more organised and analytical thinkers who are unused to your gung-ho approach. Keep your burning enthusiasm in check by consciously creating space for other people's ideas and giving them time to catch up with your train of thought.

As you've already learnt, your direct communication style can ruffle feathers, especially when you're interacting with people who are more sensitive and reserved. You're ruled by Mars, the planet of action and aggression, so it's no wonder you don't shy away from conflict, but if you're not careful, you can be just a teensy bit ruthless. This take-no-prisoners attitude could be a red flag for gentle souls and peacekeepers who are naturally conflict-averse. You definitely don't want to miss out on having these calming presences in your life, so practise exercising self-control and discipline and learn how to choose your battles wisely. Start by trying some deep breathing exercises next time you feel your Aries fire burning a little too hot.

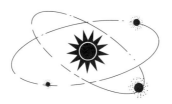

Why not try your hand at...

... journalling? Have you heard the expression, 'act in haste, repent at leisure'? Well, that one was written for you, Aries. Your instinct is to forge ahead, regardless of what anyone else says or thinks, but rash decisions don't always have happy outcomes. Spending a few minutes jotting down and reflecting on the events of the day before you get too carried away is the perfect way to keep your somewhat reckless Aries tendencies in check.

Aries across the zodiac

By now, you should be pretty familiar with our fiery friend, Aries. You know that fellow fire signs Leo and Sagittarius tend to have the best vibe with Aries, not to mention the playful air sign Gemini. Relationships between Aries and more reserved earth signs like Virgo and sensitive signs like Cancer and Pisces may need a bit more work to keep the harmony. Here's a quick snapshot of how our Aries fares with all the signs in the zodiac.

- **Aries and Aries** – There's no one Aries loves more than Aries, so sparks will fly in this red-hot pairing.

- **Aries and Taurus** – These two aren't quite each other's speed, but it's nothing a little careful calibration couldn't fix.

- **Aries and Gemini** – A match made in the heavens: classically compatible, cool and carefree, with a side of spontaneity.

- **Aries and Cancer** – These two leaders with opposing communication styles need to respect each other's emotional process.

- **Aries and Leo** – Make way for the ultimate confidence power couple (if they can learn how to take turns calling the shots).

- **Aries and Virgo** – Chaos meets order in this unexpected pairing that may well end up inspiring each other.

- **Aries and Libra** – Two fun-loving initiators with polar-opposite natures could make for a dynamic team.

- **Aries and Scorpio** – An intense initial spark, but this passionate pair needs to work hard to stay in sync.

- **Aries and Sagittarius** – One of the most well-matched pairings in the zodiac, this duo has an effortless connection to be envied.

- **Aries and Capricorn** – If these two stubborn go-getters can sync up their mismatched pace, they'll be unstoppable.

- **Aries and Aquarius** – With Aries' ambition and Aquarius' capability, there's a lot these free-spirited souls can learn from each other.

- **Aries and Pisces** – The compassionate Pisces might inspire the pragmatic Aries to think of others, while Aries might help Pisces learn to put themselves first.

TAURUS
20th April – 20th May

TAURUS FACT FILE

Element: Earth
Symbol: The bull

Ruling planet: Venus
Colour: Green

Key traits: Practical, dependable, patient and grounded
Strengths: Strong work ethic, reliability and persistence
Weaknesses: Stubbornness, resistance to change and a tendency to be possessive
Likes: Stability, nature, beauty, luxury and comfort
Dislikes: Sudden change, rushing and superficiality

Meet Taurus

For the second stop on our celestial tour, we come to the sturdy yet sensual world of Taurus. Coming hot off the heels of the high-energy Aries, Taurus brings a welcome sense of earthy calm to the zodiac. Known as much for their unwavering determination as for their love of all things beautiful, these reliable and steadfast bulls know how to channel their considerable strength and resilience to overcome life's obstacles – all without breaking a nail in the process. Think less 'bull in a china shop' and more 'bull browsing through an antique china shop, stopping to admire the craftsmanship of each piece' and you'll have a pretty good understanding of Taurus. So, saddle up as we take a turn around the pasture to bask in the indulgence of Taurus.

If you're a Taurus...

You're all about taking your time to enjoy the finer things in life, and in your perfect world, you'd spend your days lounging in a hammock, with your favourite drink in one hand and a good book in the other. What could be better?

Well, that depends on who you ask. You see, your more thrill-seeking, HIIT-class-taking, 'let's-go-speed-dating' friends might not always know how to accommodate your relaxed, comfort-seeking nature, but compromise can always be found. Let's say your sister really wants to go camping for her birthday, but the idea of itchy sleeping bags and al fresco bathroom arrangements just isn't your jam. Why not suggest glamping instead? Or, if your friends want to go on a weekend city break, you could suggest arranging it over a long weekend so you can enjoy your sightseeing without having to rush.

As a Taurus, your love language is first and foremost physical touch, whether that's greeting your work bestie with hugs, linking arms with your mum on an afternoon walk or cuddling up with your partner to watch reruns of *Bake Off* on the sofa. Closely behind physical touch is your love of quality time, and when we say quality, we mean *quality*. For you, decadent pamper nights, long dinners at local restaurants and spending hours picking out fancy throw cushions are the perfect way to connect with someone. As far as you're concerned, actions speak louder than words, but don't forget that some people need your words of affirmation as much as your warm hugs and wonderful company.

Your Taurus mantra:
'EMBRACE CHANGE.'

You place an incredibly high value on stability and consistency, Taurus, and while it's important to have a sense of security, sometimes sticking with what's familiar (even if it's no longer serving you) could mean missing out on better opportunities elsewhere. Repeat this mantra to remind yourself that change is an essential part of life.

If you know a Taurus...

Whether you've already got a steadfast bull in your life or you're hoping to lasso one soon, the key to a harmonious relationship with a Taurus is understanding all sides of their nature – and accepting that you can't change it!

When spending time with a Taurus, the key thing to remember is that they have high standards. But before you nervously check your bank balance, note that their standards for high quality doesn't necessarily mean costly. For a Taurus, luxury is more grounded in life's simple pleasures than the ostentatious and superficial, so spending quality time with your Taurus doesn't have to mean spending an arm and a leg. Think about taking them on a free museum tour where they can soak up the beautiful art or planning a picnic where you surprise them with all their favourite snacks. For a cosy night in, cue up their go-to guilty pleasure movie and set the scene with scented candles and soft lighting. Taureans are deep thinkers, so if you can show that you've put real thought into your catch-up, they'll value the effort more than most.

Taurus also has an immensely long fuse, so if you sense that the bull in your life is troubled, you may need to do some digging to coax out what's wrong. They may often ignore or bury their concerns out of determination to see things through, but this can lead to them getting stuck in dead-end situations. They may need you to guide them to the realisation that it's time to walk away – but be gentle, it's not in the bull's nature to give up, so this will be a big challenge for them.

Your mantra for connecting with a Taurus:
'BE PATIENT.'

Tuning in to the slow and deliberate frequency of a Taurus requires some careful calibration, but you'll be rewarded with a loyal and loving companion for life. A Taurus isn't going to be won over by quick words and cheap gestures, so you'll have to take the time to get to know them if you want to connect on a deeper level.

Heavenly matches with Taurus

Unsurprisingly, Taureans are happiest when they're chilling with the other signs in their element, so that means balanced Capricorn and Virgo. But steady and dependable Taurus also has a deeply sensuous side, and that's where the bull becomes one-half of one of the most indulgent pairings in the cosmos…

Capricorn, Virgo and Scorpio

The grounded earth trio of Taurus, Capricorn and Virgo all value stability, practicality and a strong work ethic, making them natural companions. Taurus admires Capricorn's discipline and ambition, while Taurus and Virgo value each other's attention to detail, organisation and down-to-earth attitude. These cosmic chums are all about working hard and keeping their feet on the ground.

However, there's only one sign in the zodiac that can match Taurus' love of sensory pleasures, and that's passionate Scorpio. Whether they're indulging their appreciation for the arts or picking out the freshest ingredients at the farmer's market, these two will never tire of each other's company as they seek out life's little luxuries. Taurus also provides the stability and loyalty that Scorpio craves, while Scorpio's emotional depth resonates with Taurus' appreciation for substance and sincerity.

Taurus and you

There's something inherently comforting about being around a self-assured and reliable Taurus, kind of like being permanently wrapped in a weighted blanket (cashmere, of course). So, how do you go about drawing a Taurus into your orbit if you're not an easy-going earth sign or a sensual Scorpio?

The first thing to keep in mind is that a Taurus will place a very high value on consistency. These steadfast and resolute bulls say what they mean and mean what they say, and they appreciate those who do the same. They also adore the finer things in life, so whether you've got a great cheesecake recipe, a question about interior design or a spare ticket to a wine-tasting night, reach out to the Taurus in your life and you'll be bonding over your love of luxury in no time.

Cosmic clashes with Taurus

While some cosmic combinations seem to fit effortlessly together, others need a little extra work to get onto the same wavelength. A Taurus' steady and deliberate approach can rub up against the rash and fast-paced personalities of fire signs, while the flighty nature of air signs threatens the consistency that Taurus craves.

Sagittarius, Aquarius and Gemini

If you're a spontaneous, freedom-seeking Sagittarius, you may feel suffocated by Taurus' need for stability. Whether this plays out in your personal or professional relationship, you'll both need to do some serious compromising to find a happy medium.

Over in the air signs, eccentric Aquarius has a bit of a reputation for being an adrenaline junkie, which couldn't be further from grounded Taurus' vibe. These signs have a reputation for often butting heads but, with work, can grow to learn a lot from each other.

Gemini and Taurus make for another tricky air and earth pairing. A typical dynamic air sign, Gemini likes to go where the wind takes them but steadfast Taurus prefers predictability and home comforts. While Taurus might want to spend the evening having deep conversations over dinner in a cosy restaurant, Gemini would rather trade juicy gossip while hopping around the newest and trendiest bars.

Finding harmony

A textbook grounded earth sign, Taurus thrives on order and stability and doesn't appreciate disruption to their sense of security. As an otherwise easy-going sign, it's not difficult to keep the peace with Taurus, as long as you make an effort to avoid things like changing or cancelling plans last-minute, not following through on promises or putting them in a position where they have to make quick decisions.

Taureans are famously deep thinkers so, when broaching a tricky topic, don't be surprised if you don't get an instant or emotional reaction from the calm and measured bull. Taurus is far more likely to go away and ruminate but, rest assured, whenever they do come back to you, it will be with a response that's been given an enormous amount of consideration.

Charting a smooth course as a Taurus

For you, life is all about stability, security and comfort. But while your slower and more refined approach to life might suit you down to the ground, there may be times you need to step outside your comfortable bubble if you want to find harmony in your relationships with yourself and others.

Your resolute self-belief is admirable, Taurus, but this can lead to you having a bit of a reputation for being immovable, especially in the workplace, so why not try allowing yourself to be persuaded every once in a while. You also hate to be rushed, but sometimes quick decisions need to be made, so you need to work on trusting your gut.

You're not as verbally expressive as many of the other signs in the zodiac, so you tend to connect with your loved ones through physical touch and comforting time spent together. This is part of what makes you a very warm and soothing person to be around, but don't forget to express your feelings, too, and remember that other people might have different interpretations of quality time.

You're ruled by Venus – the planet of love and beauty – which, of course, means you're a hopeless romantic. Being a deep thinker (about literally everything), you're obviously not going to rush into a relationship until you're completely sure. But when you fall, you fall hard, and your trademark devotion and dependability means you're going to be 100 per cent committed to that other person. However, don't let your strong sense of loyalty or determination to see things through keep you holding on when it's time to let go. Remember your mantra, Taurus: embrace change.

Why not try your hand at ...

... the 5-3-1 method? When faced with a decision, quickly write down five possible options. Then, narrow down the list to the three most desirable or achievable choices. Finally, go with your gut and choose one solution – and don't second-guess it! Practise this technique to help you get more comfortable with making quick decisions.

Taurus across the zodiac

It goes without saying that Taurus boasts a host of enviable qualities – reliability, loyalty, devotion and an appreciation for the beautiful side of life, to name but a few. But as we've learnt, the slow and deliberate bull can struggle to gel with more high-octane and free-spirited personality types. Let's explore how this plays out across the cosmos.

- **Taurus and Aries –** These two aren't quite each other's speed, but it's nothing a little careful calibration couldn't fix.

- **Taurus and Taurus –** Who could understand Taurus better than another Taurus? This is an ideal match, as long as they don't get too set in their ways.

- **Taurus and Gemini –** These two share a joie de vivre but need to work very hard to get onto the same frequency.

- **Taurus and Cancer –** A nurturing match made in the heavens based on a shared appreciation for tradition, comfort and family.

- **Taurus and Leo –** This glamorous and commitment-minded match could light up the skies if they can make room for each other.

- **Taurus and Virgo –** This classically compatible pair values and relies on each other's grounded and practical natures.

- **Taurus and Libra –** This beauty-loving duo both have incredible taste and share many indulgent hobbies and interests.

- **Taurus and Scorpio –** Sparks fly in this sensuous pair that makes for one of the most intense and passionate matches in the cosmos.

- **Taurus and Sagittarius –** The freedom-seeking archer may take some persuading to be pinned down by the stability-loving bull.

- **Taurus and Capricorn –** A deeply nourishing and solid pairing that truly knows how to bring out the best in each other.

- **Taurus and Aquarius –** Eccentric Aquarius might just push traditional Taurus out of their comfort zone in this unlikely pair.

- **Taurus and Pisces –** Both introverted but highly sensual, this is a bond based on self-discovery and mutual respect.

GEMINI
21ˢᵗ May – 20ᵗʰ June

GEMINI FACT FILE

Element: Air

Symbol: The twins

Ruling planet: Mercury

Colour: Yellow

Key traits: Adaptable, curious, innovative, spontaneous and playful

Strengths: Communication, quick-wit, intelligence and versatility

Weaknesses: Restlessness, indecision, superficiality and volatility

Likes: Engaging conversations, learning, socialising and variety

Dislikes: Routine, boredom, being alone and FOMO

Meet Gemini

Buckle up and look both ways as we whiz across the zodiac into the double-trouble world of Gemini. The dynamic duo of the cosmos, the Gemini twins have got so much to see, do and say that it literally takes two of them to get through it all! These celestial siblings dance, mingle and gossip their way through the cosmos with an infectious energy fuelled by a seemingly endless curiosity and zest for life. Gemini's quick wit, sharp mind and keen sense of fun make them irresistible to be around, but make sure you enjoy them while you can because before you know it, these easily distracted twins will be skipping off somewhere else. Exhausted already? Well, that's hardly surprising because, as you're about to discover, if you want to live life as fully as a Gemini, it really does take two.

If you're a Gemini...

Hands down, you are the social butterfly of the zodiac. Flitting effortlessly between different social groups, you only wish there was more of you to go around!

Your appetite for life is voracious, and it's what makes you such a fascinating and attractive person to be around. As far as you're concerned, juggling multiple hobbies, projects and friendships is the only way to sample all the delights life has to offer – how can you be expected to stick with one thing at a time? But while this is your preferred mode of operation, it might be something that the non-Geminis in your life struggle to understand. You need to keep in mind that what you consider to be keeping your options open, others might interpret as fickle and unreliable.

You are one of the great communicators of the cosmos, which is no great surprise since you're governed by Mercury, the planet of communication and information. You've got a lot to say, and you aren't shy about saying it! You love to express your emotions externally and find talking almost therapeutic. Sometimes, you feel like the act of talking is more important than what you're actually saying but be careful – this can lead to you saying more than you should or saying things you don't mean.

When it comes to connecting with others, this is where you shine – at least initially. You can talk to anyone and slot seamlessly into any social situation, Gemini, but be careful that your restless search for novelty and mental stimulation doesn't overshadow your need to form those deeper, long-lasting connections.

Your Gemini mantra:
'SEE IT THROUGH.'

The duality of your sign has you constantly torn in different directions, never really knowing which thread to follow. Sure, you love to dabble, but can you imagine the level of mastery you could achieve if you applied your curiosity, intellect and versatility to seeing something through to the end? Repeat this mantra to help focus your energy and talent on finishing what you start.

If you know a Gemini...

Having a Gemini in your life is a bit like staring into a mesmerising kaleidoscope of constantly shifting vibrant colours and unexpected shapes that you just can't take your eyes off. Amongst this spontaneous ebb and flow, how can you create lasting relationships with the famously flighty Gemini that will stand the test of time?

Keeping a Gemini interested might feel like an impossible task, but luckily, learning to understand them is easier than first thought – and, as it turns out, holding a Gemini's attention is certainly achievable. The key word to remember when it comes to spending time with Gemini is variety. Much like training an excitable puppy, Gemini's voracious appetite for new experiences needs to be constantly fed if you don't want them to run off into the crowd chasing squirrels. So, when planning a catch-up or date with your Gemini, go for activities that stimulate their playful, curious minds and join in as they jump between tasks or environments. Escape rooms, treasure hunts or trips to a theme park are dynamic date ideas that are sure to pique your playful Gemini's interest (and keep it for the whole day!). If such active pursuits aren't really your speed, never fear. There are plenty of ways to incorporate Gemini-approved variety into more sedentary activities with a bit of imagination. For example, you could turn your next dinner party into a murder mystery dinner party – and nominate your Gemini to be the enigmatic game master!

When it comes to having tricky conversations with Gemini, you'll have no trouble getting them to open up and verbally express themselves, as Geminis are natural communicators. The difficulty may come in sifting through their unfiltered avalanche of words to pick out the meaningful nuggets. Keep the conversation on track by redirecting Gemini back to the main issue and don't let them lead you on a merry dance away from the topic at hand.

Your mantra for connecting with Gemini:
'MIX IT UP.'

For Gemini, variety is truly the spice of life, so if you want to create a connection with hyperactive Gemini that keeps them coming back for more, keep this mantra in mind whenever you're planning quality time.

Heavenly matches with Gemini

Super-social Gemini gets on fairly well with everyone (at least on the surface) but, of course, they are most naturally compatible with fellow air signs, Aquarius and Libra. But don't forget – air and fire signs tend to fuel each other, so airy Gemini also builds strong bonds with their fiery friends.

Aquarius, Libra and Aries

Notorious adrenaline junkie Aquarius is perhaps the most obvious companion for adventure-seeking Gemini. These two will never run out of things to do together, and Aquarius stands the best chance in the zodiac of keeping Gemini's short attention span from wandering. Geminis find another harmonious match in the super-social Libra. As an equally light-hearted air sign, Libra instinctively knows what Gemini needs to feel satisfied: lively conversation, social connection and blue-sky ideas. These two together just feels right.

As a powerful air and fire combo, Gemini and Aries are classically compatible. They both love to live on the fast and fun-loving side of life and will feed off each other's frantic energy, keen intellect and spontaneous spirit. When the ram and twins team up, you know you're in for a wild and unforgettable ride.

Gemini and you

Everywhere they go, Gemini naturally pulls people into their orbit as they twirl around the cosmos collecting new friends, experiences and interests. Their infectious energy and lively personality make them an irresistible addition to any social group or team, and they'll want to be part of yours!

The good news is that, when it comes to forming a bond with Gemini, it doesn't really matter what sign you are as long as you've got something fresh and interesting to share – whether that's a tasty morsel of gossip, a fascinating anecdote or an invite to a fancy dress party. Gemini is driven by an insatiable curiosity and lust for life so, whatever you've got planned, make sure you save a spot for Gemini – they won't care where you're going, as long as they get to come along for the ride!

Cosmic clashes with Gemini

Although Gemini has some natural allies in the zodiac, not everyone finds it so easy to get on the same wavelength as Gemini. While some find Gemini's erratic nature charming, others may struggle to know where they stand with the flighty and unpredictable twins.

Taurus, Pisces and Virgo

One pairing that may struggle to find their equilibrium is Gemini and Taurus. On paper, Gemini embodies some of Taurus' biggest turn-offs: sudden changes, constant rushing around and surface-level interactions. Stability-loving Taurus thrives on security and commitment, whereas Gemini prefers to keep their options open. This pair will need to do a lot of work to find a happy medium between their conflicting communication styles.

Gemini's easy-come-easy-go attitude may also run the risk of offending sensitive souls who take things a little more to heart, like empathetic Pisces and analytical Virgo. Both Pisces and Virgo also struggle with making their minds up, which is a nightmare for the equally indecisive Gemini (who, hello, is already dealing with being permanently split in two directions!). Pisces tends to lead with their imagination, whereas Gemini chases more visceral stimulation and Virgo's meticulous attention to detail may frustrate the haphazard whirlwind that is Gemini.

Finding harmony

Creating harmony with the Gemini in your life is all about embracing the dynamic and ever-changing nature of their personality. Gemini's dualistic energy thrives on variety and mental stimulation so, to satisfy their appetite for life, Gemini is constantly on the move – flitting between friendship groups, jobs and hobbies. The trick to peaceful coexistence with the twins is to not take this personally. Gemini has a very short attention span but this doesn't mean they don't value the time they spend with you. Enjoy them while you can, then let them pursue whatever catches their attention next, safe in the knowledge that they'll be back again soon to entertain you with tales of their latest obsession.

Charting a smooth course as a Gemini

It has to be said, you're one of the more misunderstood signs of the zodiac, Gemini. The duality of your sign has led to you being falsely characterised as two-faced but, in reality, you rarely have a hidden agenda. That said, those who are primed to spot this trait in you may wrongly interpret your short attention span and tendency to change plans at the last minute as evidence that you're not to be trusted. Although this misrepresentation isn't your fault, you may want to make a conscious effort to get better at following through on your commitments if you want to overcome this stereotype.

Communication is where you shine, Gemini, and information is your currency – which might explain why you have a bit of a reputation as a gossip. You love connecting with people over shared knowledge but remember, not everyone trades information as freely as you. So, take care with what people tell you and try to be a reliable secret-keeper (otherwise, people will stop sharing them with you, and that would be unthinkable).

There's no doubt about it, you've got one of the quickest wits and sharpest tongues of the zodiac – and you're not afraid to use them. But when it comes to having important conversations, try to step back and think before you speak. Your ability to wound with words could get you into hot water, especially in the workplace and when dealing with more sensitive signs who tend to take things to heart.

Why not try your hand at...

… a digital detox? Consuming and sharing information is a big part of who you are, Gemini, so of course your phone is like another limb. But it's also one of the biggest sources of distraction that's preventing you from giving all your attention to the moment. Start by turning on Do Not Disturb whenever you're spending quality time with your loved ones, then work your way up to a full weekend of digital detoxing. You can do it!

Gemini across the zodiac

So, there you have it. That's the playful, restless, indecisive world of Gemini – forever torn in at least two different directions at any given time. As you've learnt, Gemini's voracious appetite for life finds many kindred spirits amongst the light-hearted, fast-paced personalities in the zodiac, but how does it play out in their relationships across the cosmos?

- **Gemini and Aries –** A match made in the heavens: classically compatible, cool and carefree, with a side of spontaneity.

- **Gemini and Taurus –** These two share a joie de vivre but need to work very hard to get onto the same frequency.

- **Gemini and Gemini –** Four's a crowd (or a party) in this stimulating pair that understands each other better than anyone.

- **Gemini and Cancer –** It's head versus heart in this mismatched pair that may struggle to sync up.

- **Gemini and Leo –** This naturally adventurous, communicative pair makes for a friendly, playful match that will make the most of life.

- **Gemini and Virgo –** This equally indecisive pair needs to work hard to reconcile their contrasting communication styles.

- **Gemini and Libra –** Two social butterflies on the same frequency, this light-hearted vibrant pairing just feels right.

- **Gemini and Scorpio –** Each has a bit of what the other needs in this mismatched pair and both need to work hard to love their differences.

- **Gemini and Sagittarius –** These two lovers of learning, adventure and new experiences make for a naturally harmonious match.

- **Gemini and Capricorn –** Structure meets spontaneity in this tricky pairing that may struggle to find common ground.

- **Gemini and Aquarius –** Expect the unexpected when these two get together to share their appetite for new experiences.

- **Gemini and Pisces –** This equally whimsical and indecisive pair may struggle to make their minds up, especially about how best to communicate.

CANCER
21st June – 22nd July

CANCER FACT FILE

Element: Water
Symbol: The crab

Ruling planet: The Moon
Colour: Silver

Key traits: Emotional, intuitive, nurturing and protective
Strengths: Compassion, loyalty, tenacity, empathy and adaptability
Weaknesses: Indecision, moodiness, oversensitivity and a tendency to be controlling or possessive
Likes: Home and family, art, being helpful, romance and music
Dislikes: Criticism, being vulnerable, failure and change

Meet Cancer

Next up, we come to the first water sign of the zodiac, Cancer. Appropriately represented by the celestial crab, this sensitive and guarded sign loves to make a cosy home everywhere they go. Highly nurturing Cancer is the undisputed caregiver of the cosmos thanks to their emotional depth, empathy and talent for intuitively reading other people's emotions and adapting to them effortlessly. But this complex crab also has a vulnerable side – one that they keep fiercely protected by their hard exterior. However, if you're ready to put in the effort to win their trust, once you bring them out of their shell, these compassionate crabs will extend their fierce protection to you without a second thought, and anyone who crosses a Cancer's loved ones better watch out for their powerful nip…

If you're a Cancer...

You feel things very deeply, Cancer, and you're drawn to others who do the same. When you welcome someone into your life, you're in it for the long haul, and you'll protect them as fiercely as you protect yourself.

Your ruling planet is the Moon, which embodies comfort, self-care and nurturing energy. With this in mind, it's hardly surprising that you're drawn to domestic comforts and enjoy spending as much time as possible in your home. You delight in finding ways to make your home the most cosy, safe and comfortable place possible, so your place is probably the go-to hangout spot for your social group (much to your delight, as you love to host!). You'd quite happily spend the whole weekend pottering around the garden, doing DIY or cooking up a storm for your nearest and dearest. While this sounds idyllic to you, your less domestically inclined friends may get frustrated having to constantly coax you out of the house, so take the initiative and organise catch-ups that get you out and about while still giving you a taste of the home comforts you crave, such as dinner at a familiar pub, a movie at the local cinema or a stroll around a botanical garden.

People are attracted to your loyalty, empathy and deep sense of commitment, but you don't come cheap, Cancer, and you expect people to put in the time and effort to get to know you before you drop your guard. Rather than a vast net of casual acquaintances, you probably have a close-knit circle of loved ones who you can be yourself around. For these lucky few, you're an empathetic and trusted confidante who will go to any lengths to protect the ones you love.

Your Cancer mantra:
'I HAVE THE COURAGE TO BE VULNERABLE.'

That hard outer shell comes in handy, Cancer, but you can't hide behind it forever. Vulnerability is crucial if you want to connect with people on a deeper level. Repeat this mantra to remind yourself that vulnerability is strength.

If you know a Cancer...

You've netted yourself a loyal crab, talk about the catch of the day! So, what's next? You might be wondering how you can crack that tough outer shell and take your relationship to the next level. Well, you've come to the right place.

When building or strengthening a relationship with a Cancer, the important thing to remember is to be patient. Cancers aren't just going to let down their walls and allow you to see their most vulnerable side without being sure that you can be trusted with their deeply sensitive soul. This may be why Cancers have a bit of a reputation in the zodiac as being cold and distant, at least at first. These crabs have an acute sense of self-preservation, perhaps due in part to the burden of being so emotionally attuned to their surroundings – they understand more than most the cost of other people's emotional pain, so they guard their own hearts with extreme caution. You'll need to take your time and prove your worth if you want to reap the reward of connecting with a gentle, loving Cancer on a deeper level.

Cancers are notorious homebodies, so if you're not a movie-night-on-the-sofa, video-game-marathon, come-over-and-look-at-my-herb-garden kind of person, you might need to employ a touch of creativity to persuade your Cancer to leave the considerable comfort of their home. If you want to spend quality time with the Cancer in your life doing something they'll appreciate, try inviting them to a cooking class, craft workshop or trip to IKEA where they can pick up inspiration, skills and knick-knacks to take back to their cosy home.

Your mantra for connecting with Cancer:
'SLOW AND STEADY WINS THE RACE.'

There's no shortcut to winning your Cancer's trust, but if you show them that you can match their loyalty, empathy and compassion, and demonstrate that you take the responsibility of bearing other people's feelings as seriously as they do, they'll soon emerge from their shell and count you among their precious circle.

Heavenly matches with Cancer

As is the case with all the signs of the zodiac, Cancers flow most naturally with the other water babies – that's passionate Scorpio and empathetic Pisces. Outside of the water element, nurturing Cancer can often find a steady companion amongst the grounded earth signs.

Scorpio, Pisces and Virgo

The signs in the water element share emotional intelligence, acute intuition and just a touch of psychic ability that makes their relationships so natural, easy and mutually beneficial. Cancer and Scorpio, in particular, are painted as one of the most well-matched pairings in the cosmos and the somewhat possessive scorpion values the crab's loyal attachment style. For the spiritual Pisces, Cancer's still waters offer some stability for the daydreamy fish, while Pisces' artistic side may provide an outlet for Cancer to ease the burden of all the emotions they're carrying.

Back on dry land, earthy Virgo provides reassuring stability for worrisome Cancer, and Cancer returns the favour by adding an emotional dimension to Virgo's practicality. Both signs value tradition and home comforts, and they'll both excel at taking care of each other.

Cancer and you

No matter your sign, you'll want to do whatever you can to safeguard your relationship with this fiercely loyal and protective crab; after all, who wouldn't want the zodiac's most dedicated caregiver watching over them?

A great first step to making the guarded Cancer feel at ease is by welcoming them into your home or spending time with them in theirs. Cooking a meal together, offering to help them with home improvements or simply enjoying a quiet evening in front of the TV will establish a firm foundation of trust and friendship.

The highly empathetic Cancer often absorbs other people's emotional turmoil, so they will appreciate anyone offering to listen to their own troubles from time to time. Bear in mind that they probably won't take you up on the offer at first, but be patient. Cancers may be tough to crack, but they are definitely worth the effort.

Cosmic clashes with Cancer

While some signs seem to have no trouble finding their harmony with Cancer, others may take a little longer to hit the right notes. In particular, Cancer's sensitive side can clash with more brash and impatient personality types, often found in the fire and air elements.

Aries, Sagittarius and Aquarius

Up amongst the air signs is where Cancer finds some of their most awkward matches. The free-spirited Sagittarius may not vibe with Cancer's need for dependability and consistency, and the archer's unfiltered communication style and proclivity for soapbox rants may come across as insensitive to the thoughtful crab. Pioneering Aquarius loves to challenge the status quo, whereas Cancer thrives on tradition, so these two may need to strike a balance to find a compromise when socialising or working together.

Back on dry land, one combination that may not make for an obvious pair is Cancer and Aries. Sweet and thoughtful Cancer may be overwhelmed by Aries' pragmatic approach and straightforward communication style. Luckily, they are both hard workers who would be more than prepared to put in the hours to iron out their differences.

Finding harmony

If you're someone who lives life in the fast lane, floating from one thing to the next and laughing in the face of convention, you may not think you have much to offer a gentle, sensitive Cancer on paper. However, one thing that unites us is that we all crave some form of emotional connection, and that's where anyone can find common ground with the crab.

Whether you want to confide in your Cancer colleague about a work problem, seek relationship advice from your Cancer housemate or share exciting news with your Cancer sibling, you'll always find a ready and sympathetic ear in the nurturing crab. Remember that Cancer values sincerity and depth in their relationships, so opening up about your feelings and showing a genuine interest in theirs will go a long way to creating a strong bond.

Charting a smooth course as a Cancer

Since you're generally a little pickier about who you let into your inner sanctum, Cancer, your day-to-day relationships tend to be more of a gentle cruise than a wild rollercoaster. But the intensity of your emotions – in particular, when it comes to how devoted you are to your loved ones – can occasionally cause ripples.

Those who have earned your trust have worked hard to chip through your somewhat stony surface to swim in the deep reservoirs of compassion and love below. While you should absolutely consider this a demonstration of their affection and commitment, it does not constitute an unbreakable relationship contract. You need to keep in mind that some people take a more casual, transient approach to their relationships, and they may not appreciate how protective* (*read: possessive) you can get over those you hold dear. There's a balance between cherishing your relationships and guarding them jealously, and you need to keep your possessive tendencies in check to make sure you're on the right side of that line.

For you, home is truly where the heart is, but if you're not careful you could easily slip into hermit mode. You may even gravitate towards jobs that allow you to work from home so you can spend even more time in your little sanctuary. This is okay, as long as you make sure you're not sacrificing other opportunities for the convenience of home comforts when it comes to both your professional and personal life.

Why not try your hand at...

... setting boundaries? It's admirable how intensely you love, Cancer, but do try not to get too emotionally invested in other people's problems and let them fight their own battles. Prioritising self-care, learning to say no and clearly communicating your needs are all strategies that will help you reserve some emotional energy for yourself. Remember, it's not your job to carry the emotional weight of the world on your back.

Cancer across the zodiac

Now that you've explored some astrological insights into the guarded and nurturing crab, you know that they share their compassion freely but are wary about who they let their high walls down for. Let's see how these classic Cancer traits play out across the zodiac.

- **Cancer and Aries** – These two leaders with opposing communication styles need to respect each other's emotional process.

- **Cancer and Taurus** – A nurturing match made in the heavens based on a shared appreciation for tradition, comfort and family.

- **Cancer and Gemini** – It's head versus heart in this mismatched pair that may struggle to sync up.

- **Cancer and Cancer** – This ideal match will take care of each other as much as everyone around them, creating a cosy, blissful pairing.

- **Cancer and Leo** – These two are all heart and could have a naturally loving and loyal relationship if they can embrace their slightly different priorities.

- **Cancer and Virgo** – These sensitive, service-oriented caregivers make for a harmonious connection brimming with potential.

- **Cancer and Libra** – Cancer follows their heart while Libra leads with the head, but this shouldn't get in the way of everything they have in common.

- **Cancer and Scorpio** – One of the most well-matched pairs in the zodiac, this intuitive, sensitive pair can trust each other with their vulnerable sides.

- **Cancer and Sagittarius** – Free-spirited Sagittarius and stability-seeking Cancer need to work hard to strike a balance between freedom and security.

- **Cancer and Capricorn** – This robust pairing is well prepared to put the work in to create a lasting, secure partnership.

- **Cancer and Aquarius** – Boundary-crossing Aquarius and traditional Cancer will need to work hard to get on the same wavelength.

- **Cancer and Pisces** – This promising pair speak the same heartfelt language, and the structured crab can make the dreamy fish's dreams come true.

LEO

23rd July – 22nd August

LEO FACT FILE

Element: Fire

Symbol: The lion

Ruling planet: The Sun

Colour: Burnt orange and gold

Key traits: Confident, enthusiastic, charismatic and loyal

Strengths: Leadership, generosity, creativity and determination

Weaknesses: Stubbornness, arrogance and self-centredness

Likes: Being the centre of attention, celebrations, theatre, grand gestures and performing

Dislikes: Being ignored, boredom and injustice

Meet Leo

Straighten your crown and practise your royal wave because we're about to step into the radiant realm of Leo, the majestic monarch of the zodiac. Born with the natural flair of a cosmic ruler, Leo doesn't just enter a room, they own it. Radiating warmth, grace and gravitas, it's no wonder that people instinctively gather around the roaring fire that is Leo. Unsurprisingly, the regal lion is one of the natural leaders of the zodiac pack, thanks to their perfect blend of confidence, courage and a heart big enough to share their glow with everyone around them – as long as the spotlight stays on them, of course. So, roll out the red carpet as we celebrate the kings and queens of the celestial jungle.

If you're a Leo...

You are the shining celebrity of the zodiac, Leo, and you're never happier than when you're basking in the spotlight. To you, all the world's a stage, and you perform your role with an award-winning flair that keeps everyone coming back for more.

Ruled by the Sun, your element is, of course, fire, and your passion and charisma burn with a never-ending flame, always ready to set the world alight with your creativity and enthusiasm. Your vibrant and sociable nature makes it easy and fun to connect with you and, just like the Sun, you radiate energy and a magnetic charisma that pulls everyone into your warm embrace. You love collective celebrations and the spirit of performance, so a group night at the theatre, a stand-up comedy club or just an evening of lively conversation and parlour games where you can delight and entertain your guests would be your ideal way to spend time with your loved ones.

Symbolised by the majestic lion, you are the very picture of strength, courage and leadership. You take pride in your individuality and aren't afraid to let your unique qualities shine, making you the life and soul of any gathering. Your vibrant personality comes with a seriously generous heart and you find immense joy in sharing your warmth with those around you. Loyalty is the cornerstone of your character, and you value and expect loyalty in return from those around you. While your confidence and regal aura can be a beacon, be mindful not to allow it to unintentionally overshadow others. Your warmth is best enjoyed when it's a collective celebration, so take moments to appreciate and encourage the brilliance of those around you, too.

Your Leo mantra:
'I AM ENOUGH.'

Part of your outgoing and generous personality is rooted in your desire for attention and praise from others. For you, there's nothing worse than being ignored or left out, but you need to remember that external validation doesn't equal inner peace. Repeat this mantra to remind yourself that you don't need to impress people to feel valued.

If you know a Leo...

If you're not sure whether you've got a Leo in your life, just look around and locate the life of the party, the leader commanding the room or the storyteller capturing everyone's attention. Did you find them? That's your Leo!

Now that you've found your lion, you're never going to want to let them go because spending time with a Leo is an exhilarating experience, thanks to their radiant energy and magnetic personality. The good news is that building a bond with a Leo is not only easy, but also a lot of fun! The key to unlocking your connection with the majestic lion is to tap into their love of celebration, creativity and the limelight. Whether you're picking presenters for a work conference, the MC for your wedding or the host for game night, offer your Leo plenty of opportunities to showcase their talents and, when they shine (which they inevitably will), their appreciative glow will warm your heart as much as theirs.

Communicating with a Leo works best when it's open, direct and laced with compliments. The otherwise good-natured lion can get a bit of a twitchy tail if they feel like they've been ignored or undervalued, so try to keep the criticisms to the bare minimum and pepper any difficult conversations or constructive feedback with frequent acknowledgements of their many admirable traits.

Leos are natural leaders, so it can be easy to sit back and let them take charge, but they also appreciate when everyone makes an effort. They may automatically assume the spotlight, but that doesn't mean they don't value your talents, input and contributions. As long as you recognise their need for acknowledgement and maintain a healthy balance between admiration and collaboration, your relationship with Leo will be a roaring success.

Your mantra for connecting with Leo:
'FLATTERY WILL GET YOU EVERYWHERE.'

Despite their considerable outward confidence, Leo thrives on external validation, so remember to shower your lion with plenty of praise – even when they don't seem to need it.

Heavenly matches with Leo

Generous Leo has plenty of room for everyone in their big heart, but some signs seem more destined for roaring success with the noble lion than others. Of course, fellow fire signs Aries and Sagittarius form a natural connection with Leo, but there's also one air sign that does a particularly good job at fanning Leo's friendly flames.

Aries, Sagittarius and Libra

The dynamic pairing of Leo and Aries makes for one of the most confident team-ups in the whole zodiac. Aries delights in hanging out with someone who matches their bold assertiveness and Leo relishes the admiration that Aries so freely gives. Fun-loving Leo is also drawn to enthusiastic Sagittarius as they share the same adventurous spirit and zest for life. These two fiery friends will have endless fun socialising together, but also understand each other's need for independence and freedom.

Fire signs like Leo are classically compatible with air signs that fuel their fire, so it's no surprise that Leo finds one of their most natural matches in airy Libra. Diplomatic Libra strives for social harmony in their life, which suits generous Leo down to the ground. This vibrant, social, charming pair just wants everyone to get along and have as much big-hearted fun as they do when they're together.

Leo and you

Luminous Leo has a confident, passionate and joyful spirit that naturally draws people into their warm embrace. But how can you develop a lasting bond with this celestial celebrity that won't burn out if you're not an Aries, Sagittarius or Libra?

When it comes to connecting with a Leo, it's all about spirit, so if you're a sunny, action-oriented, life-loving person, Leo will welcome you into their pride with open arms. Leo also places a high value on creative self-expression so, no matter your sign, share your unique way of expressing yourself with Leo and they'll leap at the chance to celebrate your individuality, whether that's showing them your latest tattoo, your rare coin collection or your secret stash of fan fiction.

Cosmic clashes with Leo

As much as Leo would hate to admit it, there are certain signs that may not be as awestruck by the majestic lion's room-commanding confidence as they would like. Leo's love of performing for everyone and anyone who'll listen may conflict with the more pragmatic or private personalities that tend to be found in the grounded earth signs and deeper-feeling water signs.

Aquarius, Capricorn and Scorpio

Leo and Aquarius have somewhat different approaches to life: the lion is driven by their need to seek attention and recognition from the masses, whereas Aquarius is all about independence and individual appreciation. Although both Leo and Capricorn love to lead the pack, they have innately different motivations that may create discord. While Capricorn seeks recognition for more pragmatic reasons, such as to secure a promotion at work, Leo craves the roar of the crowd to fill their heart, feed their soul and (let's be honest) stroke their ego.

Scorpio and Leo are two strong-willed signs who are aware of their considerable power, which could make for a dramatic match that sparks conflict and power struggles. In romantic relationships, the lion and scorpion may experience trust issues, as both signs can be somewhat possessive. In social settings, the intensely private Scorpio might also struggle to deal with Leo's openness and need for attention.

Finding harmony

Leo sure does live life out loud, so if you're more of an introvert who prefers to play their cards close to their chest, you may find the theatrical lion a little overwhelming at times, and a Leo might struggle with your lack of verbal validation. Try spending one-on-one time with a Leo to get to know them away from the spotlight and remember, even the brightest stars in the sky need a little praise to keep them sparkling. For the more extroverted personalities in the zodiac, finding harmony with Leo is all about learning to share the limelight. Remember that the grand stage of life is plenty big enough for you both.

Charting a smooth course as a Leo

In pretty much every situation, you naturally become the centre of attention, Leo, which is exactly where you're most comfortable. But it's important to share the limelight and give everyone an opportunity to shine if you want to create truly fulfilling relationships with others. This can be especially important in professional settings. If you're the go-to for public speaking or presenting tasks in your team, why not use your considerable natural-born talents and offer to coach your colleagues to help them build up their confidence so they can get a turn in the spotlight themselves?

In your world, communication is all part of your performance, and you effortlessly capture everyone's attention with your enigmatic presence and expressive storytelling. Just remember that substance is just as important as style – sometimes even more so – when it comes to having serious conversations, so read the room and know when it's time to tone down the performance and speak from the heart.

You value sincerity and straightforwardness in communication – just remember to listen as much as you speak. You sometimes tend to dominate conversations, but listening to understand rather than to respond will go a long way to help deepen your connections and make your interactions more meaningful.

Why not try your hand at...

... active listening? When someone else is speaking, do you ever find yourself waiting for a pause in their story so you can leap in to start telling your own anecdote instead? If that sounds like you, Leo, then you may want to practise active listening. You know how much you would hate it if you felt like you didn't have people's full attention when you were speaking, so show other people the same level of engagement, don't interrupt or talk over them and make sure you ask follow-up questions about what they've said to show you were listening properly. This will go a long way to showing others that you value their input and will help keep some of your more self-centred tendencies in check.

Leo across the zodiac

As the curtain falls on our time with the theatrical Leo, it's time to look across the cosmos and see how the big-hearted lion fares in their relationships with everyone across the zodiac, from the potentially spotlight-stealing Aries all the way through to daydreaming Pisces.

- **Leo and Aries** – Make way for the ultimate confidence power couple (if they can learn how to take turns calling the shots).

- **Leo and Taurus** – This glamorous and commitment-minded match could light up the skies if they can make room for each other.

- **Leo and Gemini** – This naturally adventurous, communicative pair makes for a friendly, playful match that will make the most of life.

- **Leo and Cancer** – These two are all heart and could have a naturally loving and loyal relationship if they can embrace their slightly different priorities.

- **Leo and Leo** – This passionate pair roars the same love language and glows all the brighter when they're together.

- **Leo and Virgo** – Virgo's slow and deliberate decision-making may frustrate go-getter Leo, so they need to work hard to get on the same speed.

- **Leo and Libra** – This stylish and sociable match loves to see and be seen – an effortlessly perfect match.

- **Leo and Scorpio** – A powerful and potentially problematic pairing with an intense spark – if only at first.

- **Leo and Sagittarius** – This joyful, fulfilling partnership will excel at making the most of the world around them.

- **Leo and Capricorn** – A pair of natural leaders, these two need to do some careful calibration to get their priorities synced up.

- **Leo and Aquarius** – A crowd-pleasing performer clashes with an individualistic eccentric in this problematic pairing.

- **Leo and Pisces** – This pair may bond over their boundless imaginations, but the action-oriented lion may get frustrated with the dreamy fish.

VIRGO

23rd August – 22nd September

VIRGO FACT FILE

Element: Earth
Symbol: The maiden

Ruling planet: Mercury
Colour: Green

Key traits: Meticulous, analytical, practical, detail-oriented and service-oriented

Strengths: Precision, problem-solving, organisation, reliability, intelligence and humility

Weaknesses: Perfectionism, excessive caution and a tendency to be overcritical

Likes: Order, cleanliness, helping others, intellectual challenges, puzzles and nature

Dislikes: Disorder, chaos, laziness, inefficiency, lack of clarity and complications

Meet Virgo

The next sign to tick off our cosmic checklist is the meticulously organised and detail-oriented Virgo. This grounded earth sign is hands-down the perfectionist of the zodiac so, if you want something done properly, look no further than the methodical maiden. The epitome of practicality, resourcefulness and order, the zodiac's gifted problem-solver loves nothing more than applying their keen, analytical mind to riddle out the best possible solution to a problem and using it to help others. It will come as no surprise that Virgos make for kind friends, thoughtful partners and valued colleagues, and whether they're planning a road trip, a weekly shop or a board presentation, you can rest assured the details are in safe hands. So, in a world full of chaos, let's bring a little order with the help of our down-to-earth friend, Virgo.

If you're a Virgo...

For you, Virgo, life is a series of puzzles waiting to be solved. Well, luckily enough, this is your bread and butter, and you love nothing more than setting your keen, analytical mind to the task.

Symbolised by the maiden, you embody practicality, order and a strong sense of duty. Your commitment to excellence and order makes you the perfectionist of the zodiac, and you thrive in detail-oriented roles. In your professional life, you'd make an excellent editor, researcher or analyst, approaching every task with a methodical precision that dots every 'i', crosses every 't' and ensures no stone is left unturned.

Your way of connecting with others is through helpful acts of service and thoughtful gestures. Because of your uncanny ability to turn chaos into order, you're probably the person people turn to when things fall apart and need putting back together, and you're very happy in that role. In your friendship circle, you most likely take on the role of event planner, handling RSVPs, travel plans and reservations without breaking a sweat.

For you, communication (like everything else) is a precise craft, and you value clarity and straightforwardness. You've no time for unnecessary embellishments that cloud the details and muddy the message. Your direct communication style is, of course, just a side effect of your desire to get things done as quickly and as neatly as possible, but remember that a bit of hedging every now and then helps to soften the sharp edges of your efficiency.

Your Virgo mantra:
'LET IT GO.'

Above all else, Virgo, you seek order and harmony in every aspect of your life, and your meticulous nature means that nothing escapes your attention. However, you need to remember not to let your love of detail and precision turn into a perfectionism that slows things down and paralyses those around you. Repeat this mantra to help you remember not to sweat the small stuff.

If you know a Virgo...

Connecting with a Virgo is all about recognising their thoughtful gestures, appreciating their excellent organisational skills and respecting their need for order – all while helping them to keep their perfectionism in check!

Virgo's love language is acts of service, so this is a great way to begin or build a connection with the Virgo in your life (especially if you can combine it with their love of organising). They'll enjoy bonding with you over any activities where they can use their natural talents to help others, so they'll probably jump at the chance to help you plan the perfect first date, organise a road trip in the group chat or choreograph the surprise flash mob for your friend's wedding.

Just like Geminis, Virgos are ruled by Mercury, the planet of communication and information – but their approaches couldn't be more different. While Gemini's communication style is characterised by output and external expression, Virgo is all about input and careful processing. This means they value clear and straightforward communication and don't have time for any waffle or extraneous details that distract from the matter at hand. When communicating with your Virgo, keep it precise and to the point and you'll have no trouble staying on the same wavelength.

One of the things Virgo struggles with most is a tendency to be overly critical due to their precise nature. The Virgo in your life may need you to gently guide them out when they get lost in the weeds obsessing over the details. This is something they will come to value in your relationship (even if they don't realise it at first!).

Your mantra for connecting with Virgo:
'SHARE THE LOAD.'

Just because Virgo is a natural and gifted organiser, doesn't mean you should automatically assume that they always want to take on the responsibility all by themselves. Allow Virgo to come forward to offer their considerable skills and make sure you're offering to share the burden of planning, checking in with them frequently to see if they need help.

Heavenly matches with Virgo

Unsurprisingly for the ordered Virgo, they tend to be most comfortable when spending time with the other grounded earth signs, Taurus and Capricorn. However, the water signs can also offer a much-needed emotional dimension to Virgo's practical nature.

Taurus, Capricorn and Cancer

Like a three-piece puzzle, the earth signs Virgo, Taurus and Capricorn all slot together perfectly. These grounded companions all share typically down-to-earth values: practicality, reliability and stability. Romantic, social, familial and professional relationships between these signs will be built on a solid foundation of mutual respect for each other's ambition, drive and commitment to responsibility. These earth signs all appreciate forward planning and working hard towards shared goals, so they're perfectly suited to forming connections that stand the test of time.

In addition to the earth signs, the deep-feeling water signs make good companions for Virgo as they add a welcome splash of emotion to Virgo's practicality. In particular, the typically guarded Cancer finds that the security offered by reliable Virgo allows them to come out of their shell, and Virgo's natural instincts to care for their loved ones will certainly be reciprocated by nurturing Cancer.

Virgo and you

Having a meticulous Virgo to bring some sense and stability to our increasingly chaotic lives is a cosmic gift that shouldn't be squandered. So how can you make sure you fit perfectly into Virgo's ordered world if you're not a grounded earth sign or a nurturing water sign?

Even if you're not a naturally detail-oriented person, building a meaningful connection with the Virgo in your life is all about showing appreciation for the care and detail they put into everything they do. Whether that's thanking them for ringing ahead to check if the restaurant had gluten-free options for you, acknowledging that you never would have made it to the airport on time without their itinerary or complimenting the historical accuracy of their Renaissance-themed Halloween costume, acknowledging Virgo's impressive dedication to detail will bring a smile to their face.

Cosmic clashes with Virgo

Not every sign will naturally click with analytical and organised Virgo. The more frivolous, flighty and disruptive personalities in the cosmos may find that they need to work a little harder to create harmony with the order-seeking Virgo.

Aries, Sagittarius and Gemini

Those daring fire signs love to mix things up, while Virgo prefers to arrange things alphabetically, so it's no surprise that Aries and Sagittarius are top of the list for signs that don't naturally gel with Virgo. While Virgo wants everything done properly, Aries wants everything done quickly, so the ram may get restless having to slow down to accommodate Virgo's more deliberate approach to life. Just like Aries, Sagittarius loves to boldly go, well, everywhere, and will already be out the door while Virgo is still checking the train timetable.

As you know, Virgo and Gemini are both ruled by Mercury, the planet of communication, but in very different ways. Gossipy Gemini's throwaway approach to trading information may be unsettling to the analytical Virgo, who tends to weigh every word with considerable care and attention. Virgo's overthinking tendencies mean they also suffer from indecision, something that so-much-to-do-so-little-time Gemini also struggles with, so this pair may find it difficult to get anything done at all.

Finding harmony

Some people just aren't about the details, and that's okay (especially if there's a willing Virgo keeping you in check in the background), as long as you're prepared to respect Virgo's need for order and do your best to not be a source of disorder in their lives. This means being punctual (*cough* Gemini), sticking to your deadlines (*cough* Sagittarius) and actually turning up when you say you're going to turn up (*cough* Aries). Virgos know that not everyone is as much of a stickler for details as they are, but making the effort to follow through on your commitments will be more than enough to show the Virgo in your life that you can be relied on when it matters.

Charting a smooth course as a Virgo

Life isn't always easy when you're as particular as you, Virgo, and you know that you need to keep an eye on your more exacting characteristics if you want to keep your relationships running smoothly. For you, the key to creating perfect harmony with the people you care about is balancing your more meticulous nature with a dash of flexibility and understanding.

Now the problem is, in your personal and professional circles, you always know the best and most efficient way to get things done, right? Well, maybe. And maybe not. Either way, your drive to crack the puzzle and get to the optimal solution as quickly as possible has earned you a reputation across the cosmos as being a bit of a steamroller when it comes to collaboration and planning. Even if it turns out that your way is the best, take a little time to entertain other people's ideas and explain your thought process to bring them on the journey with you.

One of the bigger challenges you face in your relationships, Virgo, is that you're prone to overthinking. This is hardly surprising, given your analysis-driven mind, but when it comes to your relationships, this can send you down a seriously unhelpful spiral. People aren't puzzles to be solved, so take a step back and let your heart fill in the gaps when your head can't find the answers.

Why not try your hand at...

… being bad at something new? Perhaps there's something you've always wanted to try, but the perfectionist in you was worried you'd be no good at it. Well, this is your sign from the universe to go ahead and try it anyway! Sign up for that beginner's salsa night and tread on everyone's toes. Go to that pottery class and make a mushy disaster. Join that local running club and finish dead last. Whatever you try, you'll learn that you can have unique, fun and fulfilling experiences even if things don't go to plan, and this should help keep your expectations of perfection from yourself and others in check.

Virgo across the zodiac

As we neatly fold the page on our journey through the conscientious world of Virgo, we can look back and efficiently summarise what we've learnt: Virgos tend to flourish in relationships based on shared intelligence, helping others and a mutual respect for order and precision. Let's examine how this manifests in their typical relationships with each sign (so sorry they're not colour-coded, Virgo).

- **Virgo and Aries** – Chaos meets order in this unexpected pairing that may well end up inspiring each other.
- **Virgo and Taurus** – This classically compatible pair values and relies on each other's grounded and practical natures.
- **Virgo and Gemini** – This equally indecisive pair needs to work hard to reconcile their contrasting communication styles.
- **Virgo and Cancer** – These sensitive, service-oriented caregivers make for a harmonious connection brimming with potential.
- **Virgo and Leo** – Virgo's slow and deliberate decision-making may frustrate go-getter Leo, so they need to work hard to get on the same speed.
- **Virgo and Virgo** – This meticulous match will have no trouble thinking and talking through every detail, which could be a blessing or a buzzkill.
- **Virgo and Libra** – Sure, these two can be a little indecisive, but they both enjoy solving each other's problems, making for a supportive match.
- **Virgo and Scorpio** – This is a deep-thinking, contemplative, calculated and well-matched pair to be reckoned with.
- **Virgo and Sagittarius** – A problematic pair on paper, but if Sagittarius wants a little order and Virgo wants more adventure, they could make it work.
- **Virgo and Capricorn** – Make way for this hardworking, down-to-earth pair who will have no trouble building something long-lasting together.
- **Virgo and Aquarius** – Big picture meets meticulous details in this unlikely pair that will bond over their big, humanitarian hearts.
- **Virgo and Pisces** – The fish's dreamy nature can be inspiring or confusing to ordered, grounded Virgo, so these two need to work hard to speak the same language.

LIBRA

23ʳᵈ September – 22ⁿᵈ October

LIBRA FACT FILE

Element: Air

Symbol: The scales

Ruling planet: Venus

Colour: Pastel blue, green and pink

Key traits: Charming, harmony-seeking, social, romantic and artistic

Strengths: Mediation, diplomacy, justice, fairness and peacekeeping

Weaknesses: Indecision, people pleasing and setting boundaries

Likes: Beautiful surroundings, artistic pursuits, socialising, harmony and balance

Dislikes: Conflict, injustice, rudeness and inconsiderate people

Meet Libra

Strike your best yoga pose and embrace all things balance as we drift into the delicate and harmonious world of Libra, the seventh stop on our cosmic journey. Represented by the scales, this air sign brings an exquisite sense of balance and beauty to the zodiac. These celestial artists weave elegance, diplomacy and fairness throughout the tapestry of the zodiac (neatening up any loose threads on their way through). Their pursuit of equilibrium underpins every aspect of their life, like a cosmic conductor seeking the perfect blend of notes to create harmony throughout their personal and professional relationships. The people-pleasing Libra is all about finding compromise and harmony, even if that sometimes means setting their own needs aside. So, sit up straight and make sure you're wearing matching socks before we delve into the sophisticated and symmetrical world of Libra.

If you're a Libra...

Your life is all about balance, harmony and justice, which makes sense since you're represented by the celestial scales. Not one for rushing into things, you prefer to gently weigh up your options and ensure that you arrive at decisions that are fair and just.

You seek equilibrium in all areas of your life, from relationships to style to your career. You have a natural eye for beauty and are drawn to refined environments and artistic expression. Your ruling planet, Venus, inspires your love of all things, well, lovely, and you enjoy expressing your aesthetic side through your wardrobe as well as your home. Chances are, you're the unofficial photographer in your family and friendship group since everyone agrees you have the best eye for taking beautiful photos. In your professional life, you'd make an excellent designer, merchandiser or marketer thanks to your knack for turning even the most plain and run-of-the-mill setting into an elegant affair with just a few well-considered adjustments.

Connecting with other people is your forte, and you thrive in social settings where you can engage in meaningful conversations and share creative experiences. In your spare time, you're happy anywhere you can meet new people and explore new places, so book clubs, local arts festivals and language classes will be right up your street, as these kinds of activities allow you to encounter diverse perspectives and broaden your horizons.

In your pursuit of balance, you may find decision-making challenging, as you weigh each option meticulously to avoid upsetting the equilibrium. However, your indecision stems from a genuine desire to consider other people, earning you the badge of peacekeeper in your family, social circle and work team.

Your Libra mantra:
'SPEAK UP FOR YOURSELF.'

While your desire for harmony is admirable, Libra, make sure you're not suppressing your own needs to please others. Embrace your unique perspective and remember that meeting your own needs, as much as those of your loved ones, is the ultimate balancing act.

If you know a Libra...

Ah, the diplomatic and charming Libra – your very own social butterfly and harmony-seeker. Libras are famous throughout the zodiac for their never-ending search for balance, and this is true of their relationships, too. So, how can you make sure you tip the scales in your favour to keep your relationship with Libra as harmonious as possible?

In Libra's relationships, they appreciate reciprocity and shared interests, valuing partnerships where each party contributes equally. They often find themselves – intentionally or otherwise – in the role of peacekeeper, so showcasing your own ability to maintain balance will certainly catch their eye and paint you as someone they can share that role with. Activities that speak to their love of symmetry and poise will always hit the right note, so invite your Libra to a yoga class, zen garden or night at the ballet where they can celebrate the beauty of balance.

A typical air sign, communication is very important to Libra, and they excel at finding common ground with people in any kind of situation. (Side note: this makes them a fantastic person to drag along to a networking event, speed dating or as a plus one to a wedding where you don't know anyone else.) For Libra, communication is an art form, and they thrive on thoughtful conversation, intellectual exchanges and sharing ideas. When broaching a difficult topic with your Libra, make sure you show appreciation for their insights and be prepared to explore various perspectives. Libras value fairness and justice, so try to avoid unnecessary confrontations and heated arguments and instead let calm diplomacy lead the way.

Your mantra for connecting with Libra:
'IT'S THE THOUGHT THAT COUNTS.'

Helpful gestures and thoughtfulness go a long way in connecting with Libra. They appreciate those who take the time to understand their needs and desires and put thought into their catch-ups, gifts and – particularly – words. Act and speak with intention and thoughtfulness and your relationship with Libra will surely stand the test of time.

Heavenly matches with Libra

Peace-loving Libras pride themselves on getting along famously with everyone, but of course, as with all signs, there are those they will inevitably be more cosmically compatible with. As an air sign, Libra finds a natural harmony with the other signs in their element, but there's also one fiery sign in particular that makes for a well-balanced match.

Aquarius, Gemini and Leo

In Libra's search for harmony, they need to look no further than their fellow air sign, Aquarius. Both personalities love being around other people and boast high mental energy, so these two have the potential to be a very influential power couple in their social or professional circles. Cosmic chatterbox Gemini finds a kindred spirit in super-social Libra. Both ruled by the planet of communication and information, Mercury, this airy pair knows exactly what each other needs to feel stimulated: invigorating social connections and intriguing ideas.

Outside the air element, Libra's love of art, peace and optimism finds a perfect companion in big-hearted Leo. People-pleasing Libra is more than happy to let Leo take centre stage, and praise-seeking Leo will relish Libra's vocal appreciation for their artistic expression. Together, these two make for one of the most glowingly positive and supportive pairs in the cosmos.

Libra and you

Thoughtful, fair-minded and fun to be around – is it any wonder everyone wants a Libra in their life? But how can you ensure you navigate your relationship with Libra with elegance and ease if you're not an Aquarius, Gemini or Leo?

As you now know, Libra thrives on balance and harmonious connection above all else. So, no matter your sign, if you're a similarly serenity-loving, relationship-oriented, light-hearted social butterfly, you'll get along beautifully with Libra (bonus points if you can demonstrate that you'll go the extra mile to keep the peace, create balance and go to bat for justice!).

Cosmic clashes with Libra

Libra's search for balance means they strive to avoid conflict at all costs, but even the peacekeeper of the zodiac may find themselves clashing with certain personalities from time to time.

Capricorn, Pisces and Scorpio

On paper, Capricorn and Libra seem like a good match. They're both natural initiators who support and inspire each other to dream big and see it through. However, things could get tense between this earth and air pair once they realise that Capricorns are driven by a desire to maintain control, whereas Libras are steered by a desire to maintain balance.

Light-hearted Libra may also struggle to swim in the more emotionally complex waters of Pisces and Scorpio. While social butterfly Libra craves connection, Pisces' prefer to dwell on their feelings and seeks escapism over socialising. Still among the water signs, Libra and Scorpio also make for a slightly awkward match. Intensely feeling Scorpios have a tendency to take life very seriously, carefully plotting their steps (and revenge on those who have wronged them) like a great game of chess. On the other hand, light and bubbly Libra likes to live in the moment, take things at face value and focus on keeping everyone happy.

Finding harmony

Libras highly value relationships that contribute positively to their lives, so excessive complaining, negativity and cynicism aren't going to do you any good when trying to connect with a Libra. Instead, bond over uplifting news and experiences and show support for their goals and dreams to strengthen your connection. Patience and understanding are key when it comes to finding harmony with a Libra. Yes, they may take their time making a decision (which can cause friction if you're a fast-paced Aries or an impatient Capricorn), but it's only because they want to ensure the fairest outcome for all involved. When you realise this, you'll appreciate the value in their search for balance and be even more grateful for their measured and thoughtful presence in your life.

Charting a smooth course as a Libra

More than anything, Libra, you strive for peace and harmony in your life, and while this is a very noble goal, the reality of complex adult relationships is that finding harmony isn't always as simple as it sounds. So, how can you find a way to make peace with those people and settings that might upset the balance in your life?

The main problem with being the peacekeeper of the zodiac is that you run the risk of suppressing your own needs to please others, especially when dealing with more assertive personalities like Aries and Leo. Remember that honouring your own needs is essential for safeguarding your inner peace, which is just as important as maintaining outer balance.

You're naturally conflict-averse, Libra, and you would rather settle or smooth over problems that arise in your personal and professional relationships before they erupt into full-blown confrontations. Sometimes, however, issues do need to be aired, so you can't avoid this forever. The key to navigating these uncomfortable moments is communication, especially with the more deep-feeling signs who need to know their emotions are being acknowledged. Listen with patience and understanding and respect the process – don't try to skip to the peaceful conclusion. Fortunately, you're a natural diplomat, Libra, so when faced with difficult people or situations that challenge your equilibrium, you'll have no trouble embracing your innate ability to find common ground as a first step towards consensus.

Why not try your hand at...

... the Pomodoro method? If you haven't already tried it, this is a fantastic method for productivity that will appeal to your Libran love of balance, while helping you to set boundaries (something that your people-pleasing side struggles with). When you have a task to complete, set a timer for 25 minutes to focus solely on that task. Then, give yourself a five-minute break. Repeat four times, then reward yourself with a longer 30-minute break and start again. Productivity, balance and boundaries, what could be better?

Libra across the zodiac

On balance, it's fair to say the harmony-seeking Libra makes the most effort of all the signs to keep the peace in their relationships. Of course, this comes more easily with some personality types than others, so let's weigh and measure Libra's typical traits against the other signs in the zodiac to see how they might affect their relationships.

- **Libra and Aries –** Two fun-loving initiators with polar-opposite natures could make for a dynamic team.

- **Libra and Taurus –** This beauty-loving duo both have incredible taste and share many indulgent hobbies and interests.

- **Libra and Gemini –** Two social butterflies on the same frequency, this light-hearted vibrant pairing just feels right.

- **Libra and Cancer –** Cancer follows their heart while Libra leads with the head, but this shouldn't get in the way of everything they have in common.

- **Libra and Leo –** This stylish and sociable match loves to see and be seen – an effortlessly perfect match.

- **Libra and Virgo –** Sure, these two can be a little indecisive, but they both enjoy solving each other's problems, making for a supportive match.

- **Libra and Libra –** These two struggle with indecision, but that's a fair price to pay for a partner as romantic, artistic and peace-loving as you.

- **Libra and Scorpio –** Libra lives in the moment while Scorpio plots a few moves ahead, but there is common ground to be found in this charming pair.

- **Libra and Sagittarius –** These natural truth-seekers make for an easy-going and friendly connection, albeit with slightly different communication styles.

- **Libra and Capricorn –** If this problematic pair can work towards a shared goal, they might be surprised to find they're more in sync than they thought.

- **Libra and Aquarius –** There's no end to the influence this pair could have on their social circles once they embrace each other's passions.

- **Libra and Pisces –** These two can bond over their love of art and romance but will need to put in the effort to find deeper harmony.

SCORPIO

23rd October – 21st November

SCORPIO FACT FILE

Element: Water
Symbol: The scorpion

Ruling planet: Pluto
Colour: Black (obviously)

Key traits: Passionate, intense, mysterious, emotional, perceptive, sensual and determined

Strengths: Intuition, loyalty, resourcefulness, bravery and resilience

Weaknesses: Jealousy, possessiveness, secrecy and a tendency to be resentful

Likes: Truth, deep connections, challenges, mystery, personal growth and change

Dislikes: Betrayal, superficiality, dishonesty and passive-aggressiveness

Meet Scorpio

The Sherlock Holmes of the zodiac, Scorpio loves nothing more than applying their keen and penetrating mind to unearthing truths, and in a twist worthy of the greatest detective novels, it's Scorpio who turns out to be the biggest mystery of them all. Armed with their powerful stinger, the scorpion stalks the celestial currents with intensity and passion, lying in wait to strike at those who have betrayed their hard-won trust. Scorpio's magnetic presence and piercing gaze will give you a hint into the depths and complexities of their personality, but you may need to make peace with the fact that you'll never know the full extent of their complex power. So, take a deep breath and don your deep-sea diving gear as we plunge into the dark, uncharted waters of the enigmatic Scorpio, where secrets are sacred and every emotion runs as deep as the ocean itself.

If you're a Scorpio...

Ah, Scorpio. You're known as the great mystery of the zodiac and you wouldn't have it any other way. Like the archetypal stranger sitting alone at the bar, you enjoy observing the world over the rim of your martini glass, delighting in the fact that they're all wondering who you are and what you're thinking.

Well, that's almost certainly what everyone's wondering, Scorpio, as you definitely don't make it easy to get to know you. This doesn't mean you don't crave connection, on the contrary, you seek deep, soulful connections with similarly sensual, intelligent and loyal friends and partners. In social settings, you exude a magnetic charm that can't help but captivate those around you, and although you're not a fan of being the centre of attention, your presence is palpable. You have a powerful – some might say clairvoyant – ability to read beneath the surface, and you know how to use your profound insights to make people feel truly seen, making you a bewitching addition to any friendship group or work team.

For you, communication is about so much more than words. Your intuition is so finely tuned that you can often sense what others are feeling, even when they don't express it outwardly. You believe that true interaction comes from the unspoken nuances and the energy exchanged between people in a conversation but, remember, not everyone is as adept at reading between the lines, so you may need to make an effort to express yourself more explicitly when connecting with more say-it-as-it-is personality types (even though this goes against your natural instincts).

Your Scorpio mantra:
'SHOW YOURSELF.'

Your aversion to transparency makes you wonder if other people are hiding as much as you are, and it doesn't take much for your feelings of paranoia to rear their ugly head. Repeat this mantra to help you get comfortable with opening up to people, and the more you practise this, the better you'll get at quieting that paranoid parrot on your shoulder.

If you know a Scorpio...

Knowing a Scorpio is all about accepting that you may never truly know them. Represented by the enigmatic scorpion, they are intensely private and protect their sensitive hearts fiercely with the unspoken threat of their powerful sting (in Scorpio's case, this is their shrewd, calculated mind, sharp wit and ability to hold a grudge for a *loooong* time). If the idea of this thrills you more than it scares you, then you're going to love having a Scorpio in your life.

Scorpios are passionate about their interests, so your first step to spending quality time with them is to do a little sneaky research to figure out what they're into and try to find a common point of interest. If all else fails, you can fall back on the relatively safe assumption that your Scorpio (like most Scorpios) has a voracious appetite for truth and mystery, so if there's a true crime podcast, conspiracy theory documentary or real-life, head-scratching mystery you know about, share your insights with Scorpio and watch them light up with intrigue.

True connection is not something that Scorpio takes lightly, so when you're with your Scorpio, make sure you speak truthfully, listen intently and give them your full attention (that means don't be playing on your phone while they're talking!). That said, Scorpios love the feeling of unearthing truths all by themselves, so keep an air of mystery about you and let them enjoy the thrill of the chase.

Oh, and whatever you do, don't betray your Scorpio. You've been warned.

Your mantra for connecting with Scorpio:
'TREAD LIGHTLY.'

Connecting with a Scorpio requires a series of careful balancing acts. Give them your full attention, but don't ask too many questions. Speak candidly, but don't give away too much. Show them you know them, but don't shatter the mystery. Repeat this mantra to remind yourself to handle Scorpio with care and you'll be rewarded with an intensely loyal and stimulating companion.

Heavenly matches with Scorpio

When it comes to the signs that naturally empathise with Scorpio's emotional needs, look no further than the other deep-feeling and intuitive water signs, Cancer and Pisces. However, when it comes to understanding both Scorpio's emotional and physical needs, there's one earth sign who knows how to tick all the boxes.

Cancer, Pisces and Taurus

The water baby trio of Scorpio, Cancer and Pisces are fully aware that they feel things a lot more deeply than most people, so they innately understand each other's emotional needs and complexities. Cancers and Scorpios in particular form a harmonious pair, as both are highly intuitive and guard their hearts equally carefully, so when they do let down their walls for each other, it's an honour they don't take lightly.

Over in the earth signs is where we find one of Scorpio's most natural companions, Taurus. While these two may initially connect over their shared love of indulging in the finer things in life, they will soon discover that they have even more substantial qualities in common, such as reliability, sincerity and loyalty, on which they'll build a long-lasting connection that will never lose its spark.

Scorpio and you

Passionate, powerful and with an irresistible dark side, it's almost impossible not to be drawn in by Scorpio's intense magnetism. But if you're not an emotionally attuned water sign or a steadfast, sensual Taurus, how can you hope to get to know the famously unknowable scorpion?

Whatever your sign, if there's something you're genuinely passionate about, Scorpios want to hear about it. Yes, the scorpion definitely has an appetite for the macabre, but if the dark and dangerous side of life isn't really your thing, never fear. Scorpios are inherent truth-seekers, but this doesn't just mean unpicking the gory details of grizzly crimes. They're just as interested in emotional truth as objective truth, so they'll love bonding with you over the book you're both reading, the latest episode of your favourite TV show or your latest theories about who stole your lunch from the fridge at work.

Cosmic clashes with Scorpio

While some star signs easily form a natural alliance with Scorpio, others may struggle to get onto the enigmatic scorpion's good side (which, by the way, is whatever side is furthest from the stinger). Let's find out which signs might need to work a little harder to create cosmic harmony with sensual Scorpio.

Libra, Capricorn and Leo

The light-hearted and airy Libra is not typically well suited to the intensity that Scorpio looks for in their relationships. Libra is all about creating harmony and balance, whereas Scorpio is interested in getting to the truth, even if it upsets the apple cart.

Although water signs typically flow well with earth signs, a slightly awkward match present itself in Scorpio and Capricorn. While the scorpion may initially be impressed by the goat's ambition and drive, these two signs both crave control, which can either lead to sparks flying or heads butting – particularly in the workplace.

Another strong-willed personality, larger-than-life Leo may not be the most natural fit for the dark and mysterious Scorpio. Leos live life sunny-side-up, while Scorpios prefer to examine the darker underbelly of the human experience. In a romantic relationship, a Scorpio may also baulk at how open Leo is, especially if this means sharing aspects of their personal lives with others.

Finding harmony

If you're someone who shies away from emotional intensity, you may find that you need to work hard to get onto the same page as Scorpio when it comes to talking about your feelings. Remember, Scorpios don't like to show their full hand either, so you'll have to read between the lines to get to the heart of their wants and needs – they're certainly not going to spell it out for you.

If, on the other hand, you wear your heart on your sleeve, Scorpio may quickly lose interest. Try to maintain an air of mystery by making them work to find out meaningful truths about you. Scorpios are natural detectives, and when they crack the case of who you really are, they want to feel like they've earned it – they don't want to solve the mystery on the first page.

Charting a smooth course as a Scorpio

There's no doubt about it, Scorpio, you know how to make people work if they want to get close to you. While this serves you well in the self-protection stakes, it can create distance between you and your loved ones if you're not careful.

You play your cards close to your chest and make sure you're always a few moves ahead of everyone around you. But what you consider to be careful and strategic, others may interpret as cold and calculated. You already know how to choose your friends wisely, so once you've chosen them, why not give them an opportunity to show they can be trusted with your heart? You don't need to divulge your darkest secrets (of which you have many), but opening up just a little will go a long way to help strengthen your bonds.

Ruled by Pluto, the planet of destruction and transformation, you relish change and fresh beginnings, frequently shedding jobs, environments and versions of yourself that are no longer serving you to rise from the ashes more powerful than before. This is a testament to your immense bravery, Scorpio, but it can also be another reason why people may feel like they don't know you. Whenever you start a new chapter, make an extra effort to reach out to those you care about, so they know they're still part of your story.

Why not try your hand at...

… social mixers? Okay, so engaging in superficial interactions where you have to reveal information about yourself sounds like your idea of a nightmare, Scorpio, but that's exactly why you should give social mixers a try! You have a habit of suspecting nefarious ulterior motives whenever people ask you personal questions in your day-to-day life, so practising your small talk and opening up to strangers in low-stakes environments will help you embrace the idea of more light-hearted interactions and realise that there's no reason to be suspicious when people want to get to know you. (And, bonus, you might just enjoy yourself!)

Scorpio across the zodiac

Hopefully, by now, you feel like you've scratched the surface of the eternally enigmatic Scorpio. You've seen how the scorpion tends to find natural harmony with similarly deep-feeling and intuitive personality types, but may struggle to find their rhythm with the more brash and frivolous characters in the zodiac. Let's see how Scorpio's typical personality traits play out in their relationships with others.

- **Scorpio and Aries** – An intense initial spark, but this passionate pair needs to work hard to stay in sync.

- **Scorpio and Taurus** – Sparks fly in this sensuous pair that makes for one of the most intense and passionate matches in the cosmos.

- **Scorpio and Gemini** – Each has a bit of what the other needs in this mismatched pair and both need to work hard to love their differences.

- **Scorpio and Cancer** – One of the most well-matched pairs in the zodiac, this intuitive, sensitive pair can trust each other with their vulnerable sides.

- **Scorpio and Leo** – A powerful and potentially problematic pairing with an intense spark – if only at first.

- **Scorpio and Virgo** – This is a deep-thinking, contemplative, calculated and well-matched pair to be reckoned with.

- **Scorpio and Libra** – Libra lives in the moment while Scorpio plots a few moves ahead, but there is common ground to be found in this charming pair.

- **Scorpio and Scorpio** – There's no lack of passion in this intense pairing that could stand the test of time if the power games are set aside.

- **Scorpio and Sagittarius** – If this unlikely pair can prioritise their love of adventure over their conflicting attachment styles, they will get along just fine.

- **Scorpio and Capricorn** – An easy-going pair with everything they need to be quite the power duo once they get on the same page emotionally.

- **Scorpio and Aquarius** – There's a lot this pair can teach each other about their different perspectives on life and connection.

- **Scorpio and Pisces** – A naturally harmonious match, this could make for a passionate, spiritual and deeply connected pair.

SAGITTARIUS

22nd November – 21st December

SAGITTARIUS FACT FILE

Element: Fire

Ruling planet: Jupiter

Symbol: The archer

Colour: Purple

Key traits: Adventurous, optimistic, independent, philosophical, adaptable and bold

Strengths: Generosity, enthusiasm, curiosity and open-mindedness

Weaknesses: Impulsivity, restlessness, tactlessness and stubbornness

Likes: Travel, philosophy, culture and freedom

Dislikes: Routine, restrictions and narrow-mindedness

Meet Sagittarius

Gather your arrows and fill up your quiver because we're about to embark on an epic quest across the cosmos to explore the untamed world of Sagittarius, the celestial archer. Like an intrepid arrow fired into the vast expanse of the universe, Sagittarians are born adventurers, always seeking to expand both their intellectual and physical horizons. This is why the wandering Sagittarius has earned a reputation as being the philosopher of the zodiac – the only thing they love more than taking the road less travelled is sharing their wisdom with those they meet along the way. As a typical fire sign, Sagittarius is a bold, passionate go-getter who brings their burning energy with them everywhere they go (which, for a Sagittarius, is everywhere!). So, grab your lucky flask and leave the compass at home as we go off the edge of the celestial map to explore the boundless world of possibilities that is Sagittarius.

SAGITTARIUS

If you're a Sagittarius...

Ahoy there, cosmic adventurer! For you, life is a grand and boundless journey – much like the cosmos itself – full of things to do, people to meet and knowledge to gather.

You crave relationships that are as rich and fulfilling as your life experiences and are drawn to people who broaden your horizons and challenge you mentally. Your way of connecting with others is through thrilling shared experiences, especially if they involve embarking on an exciting escapade, like an impromptu camping weekend, a spontaneous road trip or (even better) an overseas adventure that feeds the fire of your wanderlust. However, remember that not all your friends will be so ready or able to drop everything and join you on your latest fearless quest, so use your creative mind to think of more achievable and practical ways to spend quality time with your loved ones while still igniting your adventurous spirit. For example, you could invite your nearest and dearest to an international cooking class, bring them along on a guided tour of a local historical site or simply suggest a cosy night in watching a documentary about Mount Everest.

When it comes to communication, you're an open book, and that book is filled with fun facts and amazing anecdotes. Your knack for candid conversation makes you an electrifying and magnetic storyteller, just make sure your straightforwardness doesn't accidentally come across as tactless, especially when you're recounting stories that other people are involved in. Honesty is your best policy, but sometimes, the truth hurts, so you may need to employ a little more diplomacy and tact than comes naturally to you when navigating difficult conversations with your loved ones.

Your Sagittarius mantra:
'DON'T BITE OFF MORE THAN YOU CAN CHEW.'

There's so much you want to do, Sagittarius, and so little time! You struggle with turning down opportunities almost as much as you struggle with asking for help when you've taken on too much. Repeat this mantra to remind yourself that you won't be able to enjoy your adventures at all if you burn out too quickly.

65

If you know a Sagittarius...

Fuelled by a seemingly endless reserve of energy, curiosity and hilarious anecdotes, Sagittarius is probably one of the most exciting people in your life. Ruled by the huge, jovial Jupiter, Sagittarius possess an insatiable curiosity that propels them fearlessly into the farthest reaches of the universe in search of new experiences and true enlightenment.

While that may sound a little daunting, all it really means is that when you want to spend quality time with a Sagittarius, you need to find an activity that sparks their curiosity – preferably, something they've never done before so they can chalk up another entry in their mental checklist of experiences. Whether you're white-water rafting, doing a zombie apocalypse fun run (yes, it's a thing) or trying out a foreign language class in preparation for your next overseas trip, a Sagittarius will jump at the chance to join you in trying something new. Although Sagittarians are seasoned adventurers, they're not exactly the best planners, preferring their escapades to be more spur-of-the-moment. This means that when you want to hang out with your Sagittarius, you may need to be the one who actually plans it in before they wander off somewhere else.

Sagittarians communicate openly and honestly, and they value those who do the same. When broaching tricky topics, be direct, keep an open mind and try to use positive language as much as possible (bonus points if you can slip a joke in).

Your mantra for connecting with Sagittarius:
'ADVENTURE IS EVERYWHERE.'

For Sagittarius, the journey is just as important as the destination (maybe even more so), so don't worry if daring activities or spontaneous overseas trips aren't your thing. Whether you're a fellow explorer or more of a homebody, as long as you're sharing a memorable experience, Sagittarians will see it as an adventure with you.

Heavenly matches with Sagittarius

Simply put, Sagittarius loves everyone, but their most effortless companions are usually found in like-minded fire signs, Aries and Leo. Surprisingly, however, it's amongst the air signs that Sagittarius' finds their true kindred spirit.

Aries, Leo and Aquarius

For an easy partnership, look no further than an Aries and Sagittarius – two bold, pioneering spirits that will never tire of each other's company. The collective energy between these two is positively electric, and they will both just feel grateful that they've found someone who can keep up with them! Staying with the fire signs, whip-smart Leo makes a perfect match for the conversational whiz Sagittarius, and together the lion and archer make for an entertaining, hilarious and generous double-act that will be the beating heart of their social group.

However, Sagittarius' true celestial soulmate has to be the equally independent, boundary-crossing, experience-seeking Aquarius. These two philosophical thinkers will never run out of things to talk about, from the huge, unanswerable questions of the universe to their favourite hiking spots. Every minute a Sagittarius and Aquarius spend together is an adventure worthy of their shared appetite for life, and once these two team up, the world is truly their oyster.

Sagittarius and you

Effortlessly magnetic, Sagittarius draws people to them with their unique blend of humour, charm and a dash of worldly philosophy. If you're one of the people who has been drawn into the archer's orbit, how can you go about building a bond with them if you're not a go-getter fire sign or electrifying Aquarius?

When it comes to trying to charm a Sagittarius, humour is hands down your best weapon, as the archer is instantly attracted to those who can make them laugh. Like their fellow fire signs, Sagittarians have a glowing, vibrant energy that can light up even the dullest Monday morning strategy meeting. So, no matter your sign, if you've got a similarly positive energy to bring to the table, Sagittarius will instantly warm to you.

Cosmic clashes with Sagittarius

Broadly speaking, happy-go-lucky Sagittarians can get on pretty well with everyone – as long as they give them plenty of freedom to roam. This may not come naturally to the more stability-minded homebodies typically found among the earth and water signs.

Taurus, Virgo and Cancer

The dependable, routine-focused earth signs, Taurus and Virgo, like to know where they stand from one minute to the next, whereas Sagittarius rarely makes plans beyond breakfast. The archer's restless spirit may feel smothered by Taurus' slow-and-steady approach and Virgo's meticulous need to plan every detail. However, there's a lot the spontaneous Sagittarius can learn from the more methodical and reliable earth signs (and vice versa), so there's the potential for a well-rounded relationship if they can find a compromise.

Over in the water signs, Sagittarius finds a similarly awkward pairing with Cancer. Just like the grounded earth signs, Cancer thrives on consistency, which is not where Sagittarius shines. Sagittarius' blunt communication style can come across as tactless to the sensitive crab who may retreat into their shell as soon as they sense the archer winding up to one of their monologues about their strong beliefs.

Finding harmony

Compromise is key when it comes to creating harmony in any relationship, and this is especially true of relationships between the opposing earth and air signs. Whether in a professional or personal relationship, both sides will have to work hard to come to a compromise about freedom versus stability, spontaneity versus planning and independence versus commitment.

As a textbook fire sign, Sagittarius doesn't mince their words, so a clash in communication styles is another very likely source of issues in their relationships. The celestial archer is a straight shooter, which can ruffle the feathers of more sensitive souls, but there's no ill will behind Sagittarius' blunt delivery. If you sense the archer is being a little too unfiltered with the truth, just have an open conversation with them and they'll value your honest approach.

Charting a smooth course as a Sagittarius

Your independence is one of the things you value most highly, Sagittarius, and while it allows you to up sticks and embark on adventures at the drop of a hat, relationships are all about togetherness, so you need to find a balance between honouring your freedom and honouring your connection to others if you want to create harmony in your important relationships.

Your wanderlust and appetite for life means you often find it hard to see things through to the end, so consistency is not your forte. Of course, this is just a symptom of your restless desire to experience as much of life as you can, but your more routine-loving friends might perceive it as flakiness or, worse, thoughtlessness. Remember your mantra, Sagittarius, and don't make promises you can't keep. Channel your trademark honesty into being honest with yourself about what you can and can't take on, otherwise, you risk letting your loved ones down and earning yourself a reputation as unreliable.

You love sharing new experiences with people, but planning isn't really your bag – you prefer to follow your feet, not a laminated itinerary. However, as you've learnt, this may not gel with more detail-oriented personalities, like the meticulous Virgo and the stability-loving Taurus, so embrace the beauty of order and make room for a little structure to your adventures with your less spontaneous friends – you never know, you might like it.

Why not try your hand at...

... the thoughtful pause? No one could accuse you of sugar-coating, Sagittarius, and your unwavering honesty is one of the things your loved ones value most about you. But remember to actually wait for people to ask you for your honest opinion before you give it. Get into the habit of taking a brief pause before you respond, to help you make sure you speak with intention and keep your whip-sharp tongue in check (even if it means you have to keep that hilarious but devastating comment to yourself).

Sagittarius across the zodiac

We've reached the end of our adventure with Sagittarius and – in true Sagittarius style – picked up some valuable knowledge along the way. We've learnt how Sagittarians are naturally drawn to the bold, go-getter spirit of their fellow fire signs, as well as convention-challenging, airy Aquarius. Here's an overview of how the wandering philosopher of the zodiac travels with the rest of the signs.

- **Sagittarius and Aries –** One of the most well-matched pairings in the zodiac, this duo has an effortless connection to be envied.

- **Sagittarius and Taurus –** The freedom-seeking archer may take some persuading to be pinned down by the stability-loving bull.

- **Sagittarius and Gemini –** These two lovers of learning, adventure and new experiences make for a naturally harmonious match.

- **Sagittarius and Cancer –** Free-spirited Sagittarius and stability-seeking Cancer need to work hard to strike a balance between freedom and security.

- **Sagittarius and Leo –** This joyful, fulfilling partnership will excel at making the most of the world around them.

- **Sagittarius and Virgo –** A problematic pair on paper, but if Sagittarius wants a little order and Virgo wants more adventure, they could make it work.

- **Sagittarius and Libra –** These natural truth-seekers make for an easy-going and friendly connection, albeit with slightly different communication styles.

- **Sagittarius and Scorpio –** If this unlikely pair can prioritise their love of adventure over their conflicting attachment styles, they will get along just fine.

- **Sagittarius and Sagittarius –** With their equally adventurous, philosophical spirits, these two will never tire of having amazing experiences together.

- **Sagittarius and Capricorn –** Capricorn helps Sagittarius find some structure while Sagittarius helps Capricorn live in the present.

- **Sagittarius and Aquarius –** This classically compatible pair both enjoy taking their unconventional, free spirits along the road less travelled.

- **Sagittarius and Pisces –** This unlikely pair may struggle to communicate but challenge each other in ways that help them grow.

CAPRICORN
22nd December – 19th January

CAPRICORN FACT FILE

Element: Earth

Symbol: The goat

Ruling planet: Saturn

Colour: Brown

Key traits: Ambitious, disciplined, patient, responsible and resourceful

Strengths: Reliability, dedication, focus and a strong work ethic

Weaknesses: Perfectionism, pessimism, stubbornness and a tendency to be overly cautious

Likes: Responsibility, tradition, achievement, substance, structure and things that are built to last

Dislikes: Inefficiency, laziness, unpredictability, sudden change and frivolous activities

Meet Capricorn

Prepare to scale the cosmic peaks as we arrive at the disciplined and determined realm of Capricorn – the steadfast goat of the zodiac. Positively bursting with the tenacity and ambition it takes to conquer life's biggest challenges, Capricorns approach life with a strategic mindset and unyielding commitment to achieving their goals, whatever it takes. Equipped with patience, resilience and a practical outlook, the sure-footed goat navigates life's obstacles with grace and determination. But don't let their stoic exterior fool you – beneath the goat's tough coat is a heart bursting with warmth, loyalty and a deep sense of responsibility for those who join them on their journey to the top. So, lace up your climbing boots as we follow the adventurous Capricorn on their quest to fulfil their impressively lofty ambitions.

If you're a Capricorn...

You are the very picture of ambition and determination, Capricorn, with your eyes set firmly on reaching the summit of success and your sensible shoes marching you stoically forwards come rain or shine. Your unwavering dedication to whatever you've got your mind set on means that you're constantly striving towards your goals, and you have very little time for (or interest in) idle pursuits. If it's not going to matter in five years, why spend more than five minutes on it, right?

Well, although your long-term focus on substantial achievements is, of course, admirable, remember that life is also made up of little wins. Neglecting to celebrate your own – and your loved ones' – small victories may actually cause you to lose sight of what really matters when it comes to both your relationship with yourself and others. Don't just wait at the finish line but cheer for the milestones people reach along the way.

Despite your constantly busy schedule, you value quality time spent with your immediate circle of friends and family, and you excel at showing them how much you care through thoughtful gestures and acts of service. You'll be the first to offer to help a loved one move house, pick them up from the airport or water their plants while they're in hospital.

In your quest for success, communication is key. You have no trouble conveying your thoughts and ideas with clarity and precision, and you value others who do the same. Keep in mind that your desire for efficiency and effectiveness may make you come across as blunt at times, especially when communicating with less straight-to-the-point types.

Your Capricorn mantra:
'ONLY CARRY WHAT YOU CAN HOLD.'

You pride yourself on your strong work ethic, Capricorn, as you well should, but your determination to reach your lofty goals can sometimes mean that you expect too much of yourself. Repeat this mantra to remind yourself not to pile your plate too high.

If you know a Capricorn...

Having a hardworking Capricorn in your life is a pleasure and a blessing, but with all their goals and ambitions, it can be hard to know where you fit into the goat's long-term plans. So how can you ensure you build a relationship with Capricorn that will stand the test of time?

Well, first and foremost, you're forgiven if you've ever found yourself wondering if the Capricorn in your life really needs you at all. With their unlimited reserves of resilience and impressive resourcefulness, this wildly capable goat may appear on the outside to not need anyone or anything other than themselves. This, of course, isn't true (whether they know it or not).

One surefire way to deepen your connection with a Capricorn is with a meaningful gesture that shows how much you recognise and respect their hard work, while simultaneously lightening their load in some way. The tenacious and (let's be honest) slightly controlling nature of a Capricorn means they will be the last person to ask for help, so take the goat by the horns and show them that they can count on you for the support and comfort they didn't know they needed.

Unsurprisingly, Capricorn's communication style is decidedly solution oriented. When having a difficult discussion with a Capricorn, focus on presenting the facts using direct, clear and straightforward language that's geared towards finding an outcome rather than dwelling on emotions. While this may make them come across as unfeeling, remember that stoically forging on is just how Capricorn is wired.

Your mantra for connecting with Capricorn:
'SUBSTANCE OVER STYLE.'

When it comes to conversations, quality time and relationships, the key thing to keep in mind is that Capricorns are people of substance. If you want to turn this goat's head, you'll have to do better than superficial flattery, empty gestures or idle chit-chat. Oh, and remember that Capricorn has absolutely no time for gossip or drama, so leave that at home (or wait for Gemini to come over) and instead focus on bonding over more substantial topics.

Heavenly matches with Capricorn

As with all signs, Capricorn tends to muddle along best with the other signs in their element – in this case, that's the similarly grounded earth signs, Taurus and Virgo. But it's over in the water signs that Capricorn finds one of their most unexpectedly harmonious matches…

Taurus, Virgo and Pisces

The earthy pals Capricorn, Taurus and Virgo instantly bond over their shared appreciation for reliability, stability and order. Capricorns and Taureans have a mutual respect for each other's strong work ethic and ambition and would make formidable business partners, dependable work besties or supportive friends. Capricorn is also one of the few people who properly recognises and appreciates Virgo's diligence and dedication to detail, which makes Virgo feel truly seen.

In one of the zodiac's biggest curveballs, Capricorns find a highly compatible pairing with the empathetic Pisces. Despite being so different on paper, both have a lot of what the other needs and the opposing strengths they bring to the relationship end up creating a perfect harmony. A Capricorn's loyal and dedicated nature brings some structure to the floaty Pisces, while the fish's considerable empathy adds a much-needed emotional dimension to the goal-oriented goat's life.

Capricorn and you

Capricorn's impressive work ethic and ambition can often seem intimidating, especially if you're not a similarly focused earth sign. So, what's the best way to reach out to a Capricorn if, at first glance, you don't have anything in common with the dedicated and determined goat?

No matter your sign, everyone has things they want to achieve in life (even if their ambitions aren't quite as lofty as Capricorn's). Whether you want to turn your hobby into a side hustle, throw your hat in the ring for that promotion at work, or paint a giant dinosaur mural for your nephew's nursery, tell Capricorn all about your latest goal or project and you'll soon be swapping stories about your experiences on the road to success – no matter where it leads.

Cosmic clashes with Capricorn

While Capricorn can usually count on an easy and harmonious relationship with fellow earth signs and intuitive Pisces, the goat's single-minded focus and distaste for showiness can cause discord in their relationships with certain personalities elsewhere in the zodiac.

Leo, Libra, Scorpio

Ah, Leo and Capricorn. Unfortunately, these two natural-born leaders are usually headed in completely opposite directions. While big-hearted Leos seek short-term validation, Capricorns are busy building something that will be admired for years to come. However, if they can channel their strengths to working towards the same goal for the same reason, these two could be a pair to watch out for.

Just like Leo, Libras are natural-born initiators with wildly different motivations to Capricorns. Libras seek balance above all else, even if that means setting their own desires and ambitions aside. This is something that laser-focused Capricorn may struggle to get their head around, as they forge ahead towards their goals at any cost.

Another mismatched pairing may be found in a Capricorn and the mysterious Scorpio. These two signs both need to be in the driving seat which, at times, may create tension – particularly in romantic or professional relationships.

Finding harmony

One of the biggest areas of tension in Capricorn's relationships is a mismatch of motivations. Everything a Capricorn does tends to move them towards their goals, so they have no problem making short-term sacrifices for long-term success, something that instant-gratification-seeking personality types (yes, that's you, Leo) may not understand. Their strong work ethic also means that they may struggle to see the value in more frivolous interactions, which can be difficult for those who like a bit of light-hearted silliness in their lives. But, as usual, communication is the key to finding harmony in even the unlikeliest of pairings with Capricorn. Whether you're seeking to get onto the same wavelength in a personal or professional relationship, if you can demonstrate that you're mindful of Capricorn's need for structure and stability while also clearly communicating your own needs, Capricorns will respect your honesty and resonate with your drive to prioritise what you need to succeed.

Charting a smooth course as a Capricorn

There's no doubt about it, you've got big plans, Capricorn, and if anyone can see them through it's you. Your tenacity, dedication and drive are what make you such a force to be reckoned with in all your relationships, but they can also be a source of discord if you don't keep an eye on them.

You're not one for superficial or transient relationships, which may make you appear a little chilly to your more casual acquaintances, for example, your colleagues. Of course, this is just because you prefer relationships that you know are going to stand the test of time, but you should remember that light-hearted interactions can lead to long-term friendships.

When spending time with the people you care about, you thrive in activities where you're working together towards a meaningful goal, whether that's training with your dad for a half-marathon, coaching your partner for their job interview or helping your cousin baby-proof their apartment. However, remember that quality time can also mean simply existing together, even if you're not doing or achieving anything tangible. Try organising some catch-ups with your loved ones where your focus is on relaxing, having fun and enjoying each other's company without needing to be productive.

You appreciate honesty and value relationships built on a foundation of trust and reliability, but you may struggle to express your emotions verbally. Don't forget to voice your feelings once in a while and see how accompanying your thoughtful actions with kind words can add a wonderful new dimension to your relationships. Remember that true strength lies not only in personal achievement, but in forging and maintaining fulfilling relationships with others.

Why not try your hand at...

… volunteering? As you know, even in your downtime, you struggle to enjoy activities that don't seem to be contributing to a greater purpose. That's why volunteering is the perfect activity for you to do in your spare time. It's a fantastic way to get out into your community, connect with similarly dedicated people and channel your sense of responsibility into a fantastic cause.

Capricorn across the zodiac

You should now feel like you've got a pretty good grasp of our sure-footed goat, Capricorn. You know that Capricorns tend to find natural companions among the similarly reliable, deep-thinking earth and water signs, and may need to work a little harder to reach a compromise with more flighty and changeable personality types. Let's see how these typical characteristics play out across the cosmos.

- **Capricorn and Aries** – If these two stubborn go-getters can sync up their mismatched pace, they'll be unstoppable.

- **Capricorn and Taurus** – A deeply nourishing and solid pairing that truly knows how to bring out the best in each other.

- **Capricorn and Gemini** – Structure means spontaneity in this tricky pairing that may struggle to find common ground.

- **Capricorn and Cancer** – This robust pairing is well prepared to put the work in to create a lasting, secure partnership.

- **Capricorn and Leo** – A pair of natural leaders, these two need to do some careful calibration to get their priorities synced up.

- **Capricorn and Virgo** – Make way for this hardworking, down-to-earth pair who will have no trouble building something long-lasting together.

- **Capricorn and Libra** – If this problematic pair can work towards a shared goal, they might be surprised to find they're more in sync than they thought.

- **Capricorn and Scorpio** – An easy-going pair with everything they need to be quite the power duo, once they get on the same page emotionally.

- **Capricorn and Sagittarius** – Capricorn helps Sagittarius find some structure while Sagittarius helps Capricorn live in the present.

- **Capricorn and Capricorn** – This dedicated, elegant power couple will constantly push each other further to achieve their impressive goals.

- **Capricorn and Aquarius** – It's tried-and-tested versus ground-breaking in this unlikely pair that could learn a lot from their opposing approaches.

- **Capricorn and Pisces** – Pisces values Capricorn's loyal, steady nature while Capricorn is drawn to supportive Pisces' intuition in this harmonious match.

AQUARIUS
20ᵗʰ January – 18ᵗʰ February

AQUARIUS FACT FILE

Element: Air

Symbol: The water bearer

Ruling planet: Uranus

Colour: Turquoise

Key traits: Innovative, humanitarian, eccentric, independent and inspiring

Strengths: Open-mindedness, forward-thinking, intellectual curiosity and a pioneering spirit

Weaknesses: Emotional detachment, resistance to authority, tendency to overthink and unpredictability

Likes: Intellectual conversations, like-minded people, innovation, social justice and unique ideas

Dislikes: Being restricted or tied down, conformity, inequality, injustice, routine, tradition and excessive sentiment

Meet Aquarius

Can you feel that? That electrifying ripple of possibility? That's right, change is in the air, which must mean we've arrived at the next stop on our cosmic tour. Meet Aquarius – the whimsical trailblazer of the zodiac. Born under the rule of Uranus, the planet of ingenuity, these free-spirited individuals not only embrace change, they create it, constantly chasing down progress in their mission to make the world a better place. Symbolised by the water bearer, these capricious Aquarians are not easily contained. Like water flowing freely down the side of a mountain, you never quite know which way these unpredictable pioneers will twist and turn next, but you can be sure that it will make for an interesting journey. Expect the unexpected as we dive into the uncharted, visionary world of Aquarius.

If you're an Aquarius...

You sure do march to the beat of your own drum, Aquarius, and it's a different rhythm every day. Unconventional and fiercely independent, you're not one to conform to society's – or anyone else's – expectations.

If further proof were needed that you were born to keep people on their toes, just look at your zodiac symbol, the water bearer. This symbol, understandably, often leads people to assume you're a water sign, which would be logical, right? But in true Aquarius style, just when people think they've got you all figured out, you pull the rug from under them because you are, in fact, the final air sign of the zodiac.

You thrive in the company of like-minded individuals who appreciate your eccentricities and embrace your many quirks. You're most comfortable when connecting with others through intellectually stimulating conversations, so you gravitate towards social gatherings where you can engage in lively debates and discussions about philosophy, science, politics or any topic that energises you and gives you an opportunity to showcase your considerable intellect and sharp wit.

In your relationships, you're fiercely loyal but also fiercely independent, and this is a juggling act that your loved ones need to navigate carefully. You value your freedom above all else, so you're attracted to friends and partners who respect your need for space. While this need for autonomy can make you seem a little aloof or emotionally detached at times, there's a deeply caring and compassionate soul beneath your cool exterior. You're not one for grand gestures or extravagant displays of affection, but you show your love through your unwavering support and commitment to those who are lucky enough to earn your trust.

Your Aquarius mantra:
'BACK YOURSELF.'

You're an excellent team player and just want to be friends with everyone, but your desire to be universally liked may hold you back from stepping into leadership positions where you might risk ruffling feathers. Repeat this mantra to remind yourself to have faith in your unique talents and perspective.

If you know an Aquarius...

If you're lucky enough to have an eccentric Aquarius in your life, you're certainly in for a journey like no other. Whether you've known your Aquarius for a long time, or you met them last night and woke up inspired to change the world (a common side effect of spending time with an Aquarius), you may be wondering how you can ever hope to keep up with the whimsical water bearer.

The first thing to know is that Aquarians are drawn to others who share their passion for outside-the-box thinking and challenging the status quo, so if you want to win over an Aquarius, throw convention out the window and instead opt for activities that spark their intellectual curiosity and adventurous spirit. Invite them to join you for a stroll around an interactive art exhibit, attend a lively debate on a local issue or join in a community clean-up event.

When it comes to communication, Aquarians are all about authenticity, truth and intellectual exchange. They won't be able to resist being drawn into deep conversations that explore the biggest philosophical questions, abstract ideas and future hypotheticals. If you need to bring up a serious topic with an Aquarius, remember that they have a reputation for overthinking, so be prepared for a long discussion (maybe bring snacks) because they'll want to look at the matter from every angle… twice. Whether you're discussing the origins of the universe or what to have for dinner, allow Aquarius the space to express their unique perspectives and ideas without judgement and you'll have no trouble creating harmonious communication with the Aquarius in your life.

Your mantra for connecting with Aquarius:
'GO WITH THE FLOW.'

Above all else, Aquarians value their freedom and independence, so the worst thing you can do in your relationship with an Aquarius is try to pin them down. To build a bond that lasts, you'll need to get comfortable with letting them set the agenda without imposing strict limitations or constraints on your free-flowing water bearer.

Heavenly matches with Aquarius

It will come as no surprise that flighty Aquarius floats along best with the other air signs, Gemini and Libra. But as we know, the bracing winds of air signs naturally stoke the flames of the fire signs, and that's exactly where Aquarius becomes one-half of one of the most naturally pleasing pairings in the whole cosmos.

Gemini, Libra and Sagittarius

Equally intellectually curious, inquisitive and insatiable Geminis make a perfect partner for the adventurous Aquarius. These two will tear through the world trying every new experience they can get their hands on and never running out of steam. They'd make excellent travel buddies, innovation-seeking colleagues and a whirlwind of a power couple.

Sticking with the air signs, Aquarius finds a natural harmony with the balance-seeking Libra. Both signs share a humanitarian spirit and will enjoy applying their considerable intellectual energy to seeking out ways to make the world a better, more just place.

Over in the fire signs is where Aquarius meets their ultimate match in the only other sign that can match their pioneering, independent, adventure-loving spirit: Sagittarius. These two are the wanderers and wonderers of the zodiac, constantly seeking out new experiences and the answers to life's most fascinating questions. Together, they form a formidable and unshakeable bond that will see them sample everything life has to offer.

Aquarius and you

When they're not busy seeking social revolution with Libras, Aquarians have a reputation amongst the zodiac as being a bit of an adrenaline junkie, but if you're not a spontaneous Gemini or a thrill-seeking Sagittarius, don't count yourself out. Remember that Aquarius is also the trendsetter of the zodiac, so they love fashion, gadgets and all things in the zeitgeist. Whatever is new and exciting, Aquarians will want to try it, which means you'll always have something fresh to bond over.

Whatever your sign, if you're a similarly free-thinking spirit with a traveller's soul and a humanitarian heart, you'll find an instant companion in Aquarius.

Cosmic clashes with Aquarius

As unsurprising as it is that Aquarius gels with the breezy, experience-seeking air signs, it's just as unsurprising that they may clash with the more stability-minded, dependable souls of the zodiac, often found amongst the earth signs.

Taurus, Cancer and Leo

Spontaneity clashes with stability in the unlikely pairing of Aquarius and Taurus. The earthy Taurus loves routine and home comforts and is unlikely to enjoy Aquarius' unpredictable nature. However, these two equally deep thinkers may be able to find their rhythm if they can find a happy medium.

Just like Taurus, homebody Cancer may not make for an obvious match with the pioneering Aquarius. While the water bearer loves to break new ground and challenge convention, Cancer craves tradition and routine, so these two will need to put in the hard work to get onto the same wavelength, especially in romantic relationships.

Over in the fire signs, a Leo and an Aquarius may seem to be a good match on paper, but there could be tension in this air and fire duo. While Aquarians seek out new experiences for personal growth and individual appreciation, Leos are all about showing off where they've been and what they've done in return for external praise and validation. However, if these two can make room for their opposing motivations, they could prove to be a big-hearted success.

Finding harmony

As a free-spirited and independent soul, Aquarius prefers to keep their options open, and this is often a source of discord in their more intimate relationships, especially with more commitment-minded signs who thrive on reliability, such as Taurus and Cancer. No matter your sign, if you're someone who needs stability to feel safe, Aquarius will appreciate you approaching them for an honest and heartfelt conversation, where both of you can air your needs without judgement and find a fair outcome. But be prepared, if you're looking for total dedication and commitment, you may need to recalibrate your expectations of the wandering water bearer, as this is simply not in their nature.

Charting a smooth course as an Aquarius

Stability, accountability and routine are not really words in your vocabulary, are they, Aquarius? But, try as you might to deny it, there will be times you need to swallow your burning need for freedom and accept a little structure in your life, whether it's committing to regular days babysitting for your neighbour or finally signing that 12-month contract at the gym (oh, the horror).

Your unique perspective and innovative ideas make you stand out from the crowd, and you're never happier than when you're pushing boundaries and challenging the status quo – especially if it leads to improving the lives of others. While your unique, unconventional approach is one of your greatest strengths and one of the things that people admire most about you, it can also be a source of frustration and anxiety for those who don't quite approach the idea of tearing up the tried-and-tested ways of doing things with such ease. Remember to acknowledge and make room for other people's need for conformity and routine and watch how much easier it is to inspire when you're speaking the same language.

You're a forward-thinking visionary, always several steps ahead of everyone around you, and you appreciate those who can keep up with your intellectually stimulating discussions, particularly if they aren't afraid to play devil's advocate or challenge your viewpoints. But beware that this desire to push the envelope doesn't offend or isolate those who can't quite keep up with your lightning-fast mind or don't enjoy such a challenging style of interaction. Get into the habit of reading the room and making sure you're bringing everyone along for the ride.

Why not try your hand at...

... goal setting? Goal setting, meal prep, five-year plans... it all sounds horribly like restricting yourself to one path, doesn't it, Aquarius? But this can't-tie-me-down routine isn't always a recipe for success, especially in your personal and professional life. Try setting yourself some small, achievable goals and watch how focusing your intellect and energy into meaningful outcomes adds a whole new dimension to your quest for self-discovery.

Aquarius across the zodiac

So, now we know a little bit about our fearless cosmic pioneer, Aquarius, and how their typical traits manifest in their relationships with others. We know that they value their independence above all else and are drawn to other similarly free-spirited signs who won't tie them down. But what about the rest of the zodiac?

- **Aquarius and Aries –** With Aries' ambition and Aquarius' capability, there's a lot these free-spirited souls can learn from each other.

- **Aquarius and Taurus –** Eccentric Aquarius might just push traditional Taurus out of their comfort zone in this unlikely pair.

- **Aquarius and Gemini –** Expect the unexpected when these two get together to share their appetite for new experiences.

- **Aquarius and Cancer –** Boundary-crossing Aquarius and traditional Cancer will need to work hard to get on the same wavelength.

- **Aquarius and Leo –** A crowd-pleasing performer clashes with an individualistic eccentric in this problematic pairing.

- **Aquarius and Virgo –** Big picture meets meticulous details in this unlikely pair that will bond over their big, humanitarian hearts.

- **Aquarius and Libra –** There's no end to the influence this pair could have on their social circles once they embrace each other's passions.

- **Aquarius and Scorpio –** There's a lot this pair can teach each other about their different perspectives on life and connection.

- **Aquarius and Sagittarius –** This classically compatible pair both enjoy taking their unconventional, free spirits along the road less travelled.

- **Aquarius and Capricorn –** It's tried-and-tested versus ground-breaking in this unlikely pair that could learn a lot from their opposing approaches.

- **Aquarius and Aquarius –** Instant besties, these two prefer easy friendships over restrictive romances, and that's exactly what they'll find together.

- **Aquarius and Pisces –** If these two can see from each other's perspectives, they can take their wild dreams and turn them into something amazing.

PISCES

19th February – 20th March

PISCES FACT FILE

Element: Fire
Symbol: The fish

Ruling planet: Neptune
Colour: Aquamarine

Key traits: Compassionate, emotional, intuitive, wise, romantic, helpful and comforting

Strengths: Empathy, imagination, creativity, artistic ability and generosity

Weaknesses: Indecision, co-dependency, moodiness and a tendency to be easily distracted and overly trusting

Likes: Escapism, creative pursuits, nature and romance

Dislikes: Confrontation, conflict, aggression, insensitivity, criticism, restrictions and feeling constrained

Meet Pisces

For the final stop on our tour of the cosmos, we're slowing right down for a dreamy descent into the deep, emotional waters of Pisces, the celestial fish. Ruled by Neptune, the ethereal planet of dreams and intuition, Pisces possess an otherworldly ability to read and interpret words and emotions hidden beneath the surface. This is because, as the final sign in the zodiac, Pisces have absorbed all the joys, sorrows, hopes and fears of all the signs who came before it, making them the most empathetic sign of the whole zodiac. With this cosmic whirlwind of emotions swimming around inside of them, Pisces can easily be consumed by their emotional world and must work hard to stay grounded in the here and now.

If you're a Pisces...

Wakey, wakey, Pisces, it's your turn to make a splash! As the undisputed daydreamer of the zodiac, your world is one of boundless imagination, creativity and empathy – you never run out of things to keep your meditative mind occupied as you drift effortlessly between reality and fantasy.

This innate connection to both the material and the emotional is what makes you so attuned to everything that's going on around you, and your compassionate nature draws people to you like a lighthouse in a storm. In your relationships, you seek connections that transcend the surface world and swim in the unseen waters of emotion and spirituality.

For you, communication is as much about listening as it is about speaking. You have an other-worldly ability to pick up on subtle cues and any unspoken feelings that may be bubbling under the surface, making you an excellent advisor and confidante to your inner circle. While you may sometimes need to retreat into your inner world to recharge, it's important to remember to communicate openly with your loved ones and share the emotional burden you bear, as this will only strengthen your bonds.

Your way of connecting with others is through deep, emotional bonds and shared experiences that resonate on a soulful level. You thrive in environments where you can express your imagination, emotions and creativity freely, and you may enjoy trying your hand at activities such as improv comedy, amateur dramatics and slam poetry. For a cosy night, you'd love nothing more than laying out a blanket under the stars where you and your loved one can lose yourselves in meaningful conversations that meander seamlessly from one topic to the next, surrounded by the beauty of nature.

Your Pisces mantra:
'SENSITIVITY IS STRENGTH.'

Being the most empathetic sign in the zodiac isn't always easy, Pisces, especially when dealing with less emotionally attuned people who wrongly interpret compassion as a weakness. Repeat this mantra to remind yourself that the empathy you bring to your relationships is your superpower.

If you know a Pisces...

If you're fortunate enough to have an empathetic Pisces in your life – or if you're dreaming of reeling one in soon – you might be wondering how best to swim in the changeable tides of the celestial fish.

Perhaps unsurprisingly, the best way to connect with a Pisces is to tap into their boundless imagination and empathy by sharing a creative and meaningful experience with them. Because Pisces is so innately attuned to the emotions of those around them, they may prefer to spend quality time with you one-on-one or in a small group so that they don't get overwhelmed by the waves of emotions coming from a large group. Invite them to a local poetry reading, interpretive dance workshop or watercolour painting class where you can allow your emotions to swim to the surface while bonding in an artistic environment. Pisces craves soul-level connections, so be sure to use this opportunity to engage them in heartfelt conversations about their dreams and aspirations – and be prepared to open up about yours, too.

It's important to approach all your communications with Pisces with compassion and understanding first. This fish is highly intuitive and receptive to subtle clues, so be mindful of your tone and body language because they'll pick up on anything you're trying to hide faster than you can say 'poker face'. Pisces' appreciate authenticity and emotional truth, so don't be afraid to express your rawest emotions and vulnerabilities and trust that they're in safe hands – or fins – with the cosmic fish.

Your mantra for connecting with Pisces:
'FEELINGS FIRST.'

When navigating your relationship with the profoundly feeling fish, never forget how sensitive and receptive they are to the emotional energies around them. Above all else, be mindful of your own emotions as much as theirs, as whatever you're feeling, a Pisces will feel, too. Any meaningful connection with Pisces will be on an emotional level first and foremost, so nurture and cherish their gentle spirit and watch your bond deepen.

Heavenly matches with Pisces

Of course, the deep-feeling water trio share a natural connection based on shared emotional understanding, so Pisces gets along swimmingly with the other signs in their element, Cancer and Scorpio. But in one of the zodiac's biggest twists, Pisces actually finds one of their most harmonious matches amongst the grounded earth signs…

Cancer, Scorpio and Capricorn

When it comes to the burden of carrying other people's emotions, there's perhaps no one who understands Pisces' burden more than a Cancer. These two highly intuitive water signs share a unique understanding of the responsibility of being the empaths of the zodiac. These two will have no trouble bonding over their shared appreciation for art, romance and meaningful connections. Scorpios also share Pisces' and Cancer's deep understanding and appreciation for the emotional experience. Pisces also tends to get very attached to people, which suits the possessive Scorpio down to the ground, while the eternally suspicious Scorpio will have no trouble keeping Pisces' overly trusting nature in check.

While they may not appear to have much in common at first glance, a closer look at Pisces and Capricorn will reveal one of the zodiac's most pleasant pairings. The disciplined goat's unwavering patience is perfectly matched to the floaty, indecisive fish, while Pisces' appreciation for the emotional side of the human experience provides a perfect counterbalance to the goal-oriented Capricorn.

Pisces and you

Gentle, sensitive Pisces adds a unique, empathetic voice to any social group, and it's one to be cherished and protected. But if it takes you a little longer to make emotional connections, how else can you connect with the feelings-first fish?

A daydreaming Pisces constantly drifts between the reality and fantasy realms, allowing their imagination to blur the lines freely. It's hardly surprising, then, that Pisces are often huge fans of books, TV shows and movies that offer them this same level of escapism. If there's a high fantasy, dystopian or sci-fi franchise you can't stop talking about, share it with your Pisces and bond over the rich worldbuilding and creativity that appeals so perfectly to Pisces' boundless imagination.

Cosmic clashes with Pisces

While Pisces seems to be a natural fit with the rest of the water element signs and the patient Capricorn, they may struggle with the more casual and flighty personality types in the zodiac.

Aries, Gemini and Libra

An energetic, ambitious Aries is not a natural companion for Pisces, as these two are moving at completely different speeds and in completely different directions. Go-with-the-flow Pisces lets the tide carry them wherever it goes, while the impatient Aries brazenly forges ahead at a million miles an hour. When it comes to communication, these two need to work really hard to get on the same page, as the ram's trademark bold communication style may overwhelm the sensitive fish.

Over in the air signs, light-hearted Libra may struggle with the emotional depth required in their relationship with Pisces. While Pisces prefers to get lost in their thoughts and imaginary worlds, Libra prefers to spread their social butterfly wings and live in the moment. However, both of these signs crave connection and emotional harmony, so they may be able to find compromise if they set their hearts to it.

On paper, Gemini and Pisces seem like they have a lot in common. They both share a dual symbol that's pulling them in opposite directions (although the two fish are pulling Pisces towards the material and spiritual realms, while the twins are just pulling Gemini to two separate parties). But these similarities are exactly what often makes Pisces and Gemini incompatible – if left to their own devices, this indecisive pair would never make their minds up about anything!

Finding harmony

While Pisces' gentle pace suits them just fine, it can certainly cause tensions in their relationships with the more fast-paced, action-oriented, go-getter personalities in their lives. If this sounds like you, remember that the key to harmony is understanding that there's a time and a place for both approaches. Respect Pisces' emotional process, create the space for honest, heartfelt communication and you'll find a compromise in no time.

Charting a smooth course as a Pisces

You're definitely not one to rush through life, Pisces, so perhaps it's not surprising that you're the final sign in the zodiac. While everyone else is rushing around, you prefer to go with the flow, following the currents of your emotions and allowing each experience to wash over you in its own time.

However, in today's fast-paced world, you may need to force yourself to pick up the pace or you'll risk getting left behind. This is particularly evident in the workplace, where you may find it difficult to assert yourself in more confrontational conversations because you are so naturally considerate of other people's feelings. Remember your mantra and remind yourself that being assertive doesn't mean being unfeeling. You have an otherworldly ability to channel your empathy to diffuse tensions, find creative solutions and bring much-needed harmony to even the most challenging interactions. Use it!

Everyone in your life knows they can come to you for comfort, solace and understanding on a deeply emotional level, so you're probably the go-to shoulder to cry on in your family or friendship group. However, sometimes the depths of your empathy can leave you feeling overwhelmed by the weight of other people's feelings. Your loved ones may not realise that you go around soaking up everyone else's emotions like a big celestial sponge, so you have to remember to wring yourself out once in a while. Carve out some quality time for yourself where you can recharge and reconnect with your own emotional energy.

Why not try your hand at...

... meditation? You're known as the daydreamer of the zodiac, Pisces, and it's not hard to understand why. The two fish in your symbol are constantly dividing your attention between reality and fantasy, which is why you have such difficulty staying grounded in the here and now. Meditation is a fantastic practice to help you learn to stay present, plus, it also provides you with the perfect peaceful outlet to process your own emotions instead of focusing on everyone else's.

Pisces across the zodiac

As we slowly wake from our tour of the dreamy world of Pisces, we can look back on what we've learnt about the most empathetic sign in the zodiac. We know that the compassionate fish seeks out soulful companions on their emotional frequency and may struggle to find harmony with more volatile personality types. So how does this play out on the grand stage of the cosmos?

- **Pisces and Aries** – The compassionate Pisces might inspire the pragmatic Aries to think of others, while Aries might help Pisces to put themselves first.

- **Pisces and Taurus** – Both introverted but highly sensual, this is a bond based on self-discovery and mutual respect.

- **Pisces and Gemini** – This equally whimsical and indecisive pair may struggle to make their minds up, especially about how best to communicate.

- **Pisces and Cancer** – This promising pair speak the same heartfelt language, and the structured crab can make the dreamy fish's dreams come true.

- **Pisces and Leo** – This pair may bond over their boundless imaginations, but the action-oriented lion may get frustrated with the dreamy fish.

- **Pisces and Virgo** – The fish's dreamy nature can be inspiring or confusing to ordered, grounded Virgo, so these two need to work hard to speak the same language.

- **Pisces and Libra** – These two can bond over their love of art and romance but will need to put in the effort to find deeper harmony.

- **Pisces and Scorpio** – A naturally harmonious match, this could make for a passionate, spiritual and deeply connected pair.

- **Pisces and Sagittarius** – This unlikely pair may struggle to communicate but challenge each other in ways that help them grow.

- **Pisces and Capricorn** – Pisces values Capricorn's loyal, steady nature while Capricorn is drawn to supportive Pisces' intuition in this harmonious match.

- **Pisces and Aquarius** – If these two can see from each other's perspectives, they can take their wild dreams and turn them into something amazing.

- **Pisces and Pisces** – These two will be there for each other emotionally more than anyone else can in this deeply fulfilling meeting of minds.

CONCLUSION

As we come to the end of our journey through the stars, you should now be equipped with a cosmic toolkit positively bursting with astrological insights to help you feel enlightened, empowered and inspired to nourish all your relationships. As well as exploring how the typical characteristics of your sign manifest in your personal and professional relationships, you've also hopefully gained a little understanding into how various astrological influences might drive the words, thoughts and actions of your loved ones.

Across these pages, we've seen how the fiery determination of Aries motivates them to take charge and boldly lead the way, while the steadfast Taurus creates a foundation of comfort and stability in their relationships. We've been entertained by the quick-witted versatility of Gemini and soothed by the compassion offered by Cancer. We've given Leo a standing ovation for their magnetic charisma and marvelled at the meticulous precision with which Virgo creates order and reliability in their life. After embracing the well-balanced, harmonious world of Libra, we've dived into the mysterious depths of Scorpio's intense emotions. We've celebrated the boundless optimism and sense of adventure that Sagittarius brings to the table and admired the unwavering ambition of Capricorn. Finally, we've been illuminated by Aquarius' visionary glow and enveloped in the infinitely empathetic waters of Pisces, who showed us that compassion and understanding are the keys to any successful relationship.

As you go forward and apply these insights to your everyday relationships and interactions, remember that, while astrology can be a great way to understand each other a little better (and couldn't the world do with a little more understanding?), cosmic compatibility is just one piece of a much larger puzzle. Fulfilling relationships require effort, respect and compassion, no matter how compatible your zodiac signs might be.

Hopefully you have discovered some tips and tricks in this book to help nourish your relationships so they can blossom into strong, long-lasting bonds, whether that be at work, within your friendship group, your family or with a romantic partner. Whatever your sign, embrace every wonderful quirk which makes up your cosmic blueprint. Remember, meaningful connections – both new and old – can be created and strengthened any time when we switch our focus to better understanding others.